# The Elevation

## of the

# Femalepreneur

### Volume 3

Typeset by Fuzzy Flamingo
www.fuzzyflamingo.co.uk

Dan Lord at Forecast Designs
Claire newman-williams photography
Gary Chuter: Shuttermadness.co.uk

A catalogue for this book is available from the British
Library.

Welcome to this book of wonderful inspirational stories of twenty-three incredible femalepreneurs.

These women have all come together to show you that anything is possible.

This book series comes from a place of love, faith and hope, to show you that every single person's journey is different, and you really can get through whatever curveballs the universe throws your way.

Keep your head held high, your femalepreneur pants pulled up, and trust that everything happens for you and for your journey!

Sending you lots of love and light and we hope you enjoy this magnificent read,

Love The Femalepreneurs!

# CONTENTS

# BE THE YOU
# YOU WERE BORN TO BE

*Rachel Jobson*

*I dedicate this chapter to everyone who has been a part of my
life; the ones who told me I couldn't do it, the ones who doubted
me, the ones who helped to shrink my inner self because "she
wasn't good enough" and those who inflicted pain and trauma;
because of you I am the woman I am today. And also to the
ones who stuck around, the ones who helped to build me up,
the ones who allowed me to become and show my real self and
loved me for me, for you I am eternally grateful.*

*I also dedicate this chapter to every woman who has ever felt
lost, stuck and afraid to be her true self.*

*This is for you; this is your time to rise.*

Have you ever felt lost?

Have you ever wondered who you really are?

That is exactly how I have felt my whole life.

I grew up scared to show the real me for fear of
judgement and opinions.

I had always been misunderstood and I never really

felt like I fit in. I was a people pleaser. I would be, do and say what I thought people wanted, what would make them happy and what would get me picked on the least. I wanted to fit in and always knew I was outside of the norm.

I never really knew what I wanted to be growing up, I flitted to all different things, but it always involved helping people. I knew this was where my heart was, and I dreamed of making something of myself one day.

During high school, this dream became more and more distant as the years went on.

It was more acceptable to mess around, socialise and not be one of the geeks that I so badly wanted to be. Although I tried to fit in, I was still bullied most of my school years for multiple different reasons and my confidence was shot.

Even my teachers ridiculed me and, even though inside I wanted to achieve well and succeed in life, I no longer believed I could.

I was just fourteen when I was sexually assaulted and, even though I covered it well and, for a long time, told no one, it had broken me inside. I lost my trust in people and valued myself even less than I had before. From the outside it is easy to tell an assault victim that it wasn't their fault, but in reality, it is not that simple. Every victim I know blamed themselves and I was no exception. I felt used but also believed that I had allowed this to happen, so retaliated the only way I knew how, to give men what they wanted, only now I was in control.

THE ELEVATION OF THE *Femalepreneur*

This led me down a dangerous and unforgiving path of drink, parties and sex and even further from the path I had always wanted to take.

Over the following two years, I partied hard and was ridiculed harder. Now they had more ammunition. My recently discovered sexuality and the fact that I stood out as different because I was loud and seemingly carefree just meant I was an easier target and the bullying progressed.

At sixteen, I decided to drop out. I was doing A levels, or trying to, whilst also trying to fit in and pretend the names and bullying didn't bother me. I was skipping lessons left, right and centre and I was falling behind. I knew I wasn't where I wanted to be or doing what I wanted to do but I had no vision of an end goal. I decided to take a year out to think about my future, make better decisions and just generally figure my life out. Everyone said I was failing, I wouldn't make anything of myself and shouldn't just give up, but I knew if I carried on, I would only fail anyway. I needed to break away and start afresh.

As it turned out, life figured itself out for me, and at seventeen I became a mum to a beautiful baby boy. One of the scariest and happiest moments of my life all rolled into one. I felt alive and whole and so full of love but, of course, the tirade continued. Again, of course, I was told I had failed, I wouldn't make anything of myself and on top of that the 'young mum' judgements flew in. A young, council estate mum on benefits would be my life.

I had been working a few hours a week in a shop and was still living at home. I didn't have much, but I was determined to do all I could from then on to give this beautiful human everything he deserved.

Over the years I have suffered sexual, physical and mental abuse. I have been ridiculed for my looks, sexuality, dress sense and just about anything else on top. I have been made to believe I am not good enough, as a parent or a person. Experiencing abusive relationships meant I had again lost my control, this time mentally as well as physically. Eventually I reached my lowest low. I was done. I had nothing. I was nothing. This was my breaking point.

By this point I was a mummy to two beautiful babies and had no idea what to do or where to go with my life.

A year later, in my early twenties, I met my husband and, even then, I couldn't truly open up and let myself out. To be honest, I wasn't even sure who that was anymore. I had spent so long trying to be what I thought everyone wanted me to be and doing what everyone wanted me to do, I didn't even know what I was hiding, I had lost all sight of who I was or wanted to be. I didn't even know what I liked. I was lost. I was just surviving and doing the best job I could as a mum. I had zero confidence and most of my actions and behaviours were conditioned from the baggage I carried so heavily from my past. Rather than trying to take back the power I had surrendered, I was living behind walls of protection.

Years passed, and we had become a family of seven. Five amazing children, a home, a beautiful wedding and

I didn't feel quite so broken anymore; it's funny how love can heal you. I still had little confidence and was a massive people pleaser, but I was much happier in my life, there was just something missing.

That need so many mothers have but don't talk about.

The need for something for me.

So many parents feel guilty for needing something for them, like their worlds should revolve around their children and only them. But our worlds do revolve around them, everything we do, think, say, they are there in our every thought, but that doesn't mean we can't still be us.

I had been Mum for eleven years, from the early age of seventeen, and even before that I had never really been me or done anything for myself. The question was... what??

I didn't know what I wanted to do, I didn't know what I liked, I certainly had no idea where to start. I just knew I needed to be Rachel as well as Mum, she needed her place in my life too.

I knew I wanted to be home with my family, I knew I didn't want to give up the time I shared with them and I also knew I loved helping people. How could I tie all of that into something? I didn't know until something came along that excited me.

I had been using some new products, recommended to me by a friend to sort out my horrendous skin, and I fell in love with them! My friend then told me about the business. It sounded amazing! Although I knew nothing about beauty and had no idea where to start, the idea of recognition, free products and being able to help others with their skin in the same way the products had helped me excited me. I took the leap and started my very own business in network marketing.

I loved it!!

Getting to know the products, getting to try them out and share my love for them was just amazing and so much fun. Plus, I loved the social side too. I was meeting new people and making new friends. Don't get me wrong, my confidence was not fixed overnight and at the start there was a lot I wouldn't do. I was incredibly shy and wouldn't show myself at all. I would always make sure my video and audio was off on Zoom call meetings, blaming the fact the kids were up and noisy, although this was barely ever true. I used to sit and see others on social media sharing videos and going live and inside I was dying to do the same, but I feared putting myself in a vulnerable position and opening myself up to ridicule once again.

I often looked at the top and dreamed of making this into something incredible for me and my family but, as always, I held back. Those old limiting beliefs were still there. I wasn't good enough.

After my first year in the business, I attended one of our annual conferences and WOW I had never seen anything like it. I didn't see "people at the top" and "people at the bottom", I saw people from all walks of life coming together to build each other up, support each other, celebrate each other's successes and it still makes me emotional now thinking about that moment I felt the fire inside me for the first time. This wasn't about having to be a certain way; everyone was accepted for who they were. This wasn't about getting to the top; this was about building a community where everyone could be their true selves and we would all be holding each other up. Something inside me clicked. This was what I wanted to build. A community of no judgement, no ridicule; just love, support and togetherness.

When I got home, I was on a mission, the passion was high and I went live for the first time. I fought the fear and put myself out there. I took on training and started talking to more people. It wasn't long before I started building my own team and soon gained my manager title. I'd done it! I was making it happen! Now to keep going, I didn't want to stop there... only it didn't happen like that.

I could only seem to get so far. I spent a year yo-yoing up and down, my team grew but not massively, I plodded along slow and steady, that was okay, but I began to notice that, no matter what I did, I never got higher than that certain point. I was really struggling with self-belief and having the confidence to build and run a team.

A part of me really wanted to fly, I knew it was what I wanted, I knew it was all my dreams come true. I could help people like I had always wanted to whilst being home and present with my family, whilst also bringing in an income. The other part of me didn't feel the same. The other part was rooted firmly to the ground, scared and full of self-doubt.

Everything anyone had ever said came flooding back, I would never make anything of myself, I was a failure, I would only be 'just' Mum, and it all boiled down to one crucial thing… I WAS TERRIFIED TO SHOW THE REAL ME.

That was the moment I decided it was now or never.

I searched social media for help, attended a few courses and took on new training.

I embraced everything I was learning and implemented it all within my business.

At the end of 2019, I saw a video talking about being an energetic match. I was intrigued, it made so much sense. The more I listened to this video about needing to believe in yourself and your goals, about being stuck, about feeling like you deserve it, the more I resonated with everything these women were saying. Every word rang true.

All the baggage I had previously carried was still there. I had tried to cover it up, but really, underneath it all, I believed I didn't deserve success and I just wasn't good enough.

I dedicated 2020 to changing that.

I worked with an incredible mindset coach (the one from the video), had timeline therapy on my negative emotions and limiting beliefs and worked massively on myself. Instead of covering the baggage, I chucked it out of the window!

I filled myself with positive affirmations, positive reframes and started journaling, something I highly recommend to everyone, it's a game changer!

I also attended courses and read books about network marketing, social media, putting yourself out there and how to stop worrying what other people think, something else I massively recommend to everyone.

This past year everything has changed for me. Not only have I freed myself from all the baggage that weighed me down, but I have found out who I am and embraced her. I have the confidence to deliver training to my team and help and support them in their goals. I love nothing more than helping others grow and get to where they want to be.

Last year my business went from strength to strength and grew by 450%; I am finally building my dream. The community of people from all walks of life coming together to help, support, empower and celebrate each other. And I'm not stopping there, I will continue to build the community and help as many people as I can to be themselves and achieve what they truly desire because everyone deserves to.

Growing up I never fit in but now there is a whole tribe of us all fitting together.

I used to tell myself that I would prove everyone wrong, but really, I never believed it until now; now I *know* I will. The young mum who dropped out of school is now a not-so-young mum of five amazing children and is running a successful business from home just by being her true authentic self.

So here is my message to you: don't hide. You are fabulous, amazing, incredible and worth all the love in the world. I'm not saying it's easy, but I am here to tell you that it is beyond worth it. Stop trying to fit in; when you embrace who you truly are you will find a whole tribe of people that love you just as you are.

Someone once told me that the probability of you being born on the day you were born, with the DNA you have and all those wonderful things inside you is one in 400 trillion!

You are a miracle!!

All those feelings you have, those dreams, desires, wants, needs, all those little quirks, they were given to you for a reason. They are you. They are your purpose. Don't hide them, embrace them, love them, own them, they are yours!

Don't live a mundane life, go out there and get the life that was meant for you.

Be the you you were born to be!

★★★

You can find Rachel here:

https://www.facebook.com/rachel.jobson13
https://www.facebook.com/groups/bodyshopwithrachel/

# I Didn't Choose This!
## Tracey Blake

*This is for Luke, who showed me that different isn't wrong and that I am braver than I thought.*

Okay. Decision time. Do you really want to end everything? Because now is your chance. The lorry heading towards you will absolutely do the job.

I was in the toughest period of my life. A time of adventure, which just hadn't worked as it should. I didn't choose to be so unhappy that I was ready to end my life. What had led me to this?

As a fit, active seventeen year old, who had grown up in a military family, what else was I going to do but join the Women's Royal Naval Service? The WRNS was the perfect hiding place for a shy, naïve girl with no confidence. I had grown up with a very domineering, but lovely, father, and a mother who also lacked confidence. I chose boarding school and had a very positive experience there, but I was cocooned. So, the WRNS was the perfect career for me. It offered the personal development I so desperately needed and the sports and fitness that I loved. I was never good at sports, I didn't have the confidence for that, but I did enjoy it. I have always been a mountaineer; walking and climbing in places like the Lake District with my dad. It was our thing, so I needed to be fit. I discovered a love of long-distance running. I didn't need to be part of a team and I could run anywhere I was based. I can remember getting a new pair of trainers, deciding to pack up my tiny tent and head off to a campsite in Dorset, doing a ten-mile clifftop run the next morning and then heading home. These were my joys in life.

When I was eighteen, I got my dream posting in Norway. I learnt both cross country and downhill skiing and these became one of the greatest joys in my life. What's more, I was quite good at it too. It was the year of the Lillehammer Olympics and I got the chance to ski the Olympic slalom run. It was amazing, although some of the route was done upside down and on my backside! Life was good, but I was lonely. Since being a young girl, I had never wanted to get married or have children. It was just not something I wanted. Now I look back, I don't think I ever felt that I deserved to be loved by anyone other than my parents. They didn't get a choice, they had to love me! I did meet someone and, after a while, we discussed children and both agreed that we didn't want them yet.

In the summer of 1994, I went out to the Alps with a joint service team. It was a climbing trip, and my dad wasn't going. I was being "big brothered" by fourteen Royal Marines. I had a lot of fun but unfortunately picked up an injury that would ultimately change my life for ever. I rescued two guys from a collapsing cliff by physically lifting them off it. At the time, it seemed that I had strained an already damaged arm but some time later I discovered that I had damaged my spine and would be in pain with it for the rest of my life.

In 1996, my brother's partner fell pregnant and I think this changed things for the man in my life. He decided that he wanted children and he wasn't willing to wait anymore. At this point he was serving abroad, and I was back in the UK. He rang me and told me that he had cancer and that if we didn't have children straight away, we would never have them. This was a tough time. I knew that I didn't want children yet. If I had a child, I couldn't be an absent parent and so would have to give up my career, and I wasn't really ready to do that. Not that long before this, I had discovered that my fiancé had thousands of pounds of debt that he hadn't told me about. I had used all of my savings and taken out a loan to pay the rest off. We were still paying that loan and had no back up savings to use.

Five months into my pregnancy, my mum discovered that there had never been any cancer. It was just another lie. This, on top of the debt, was the last straw. We paid the final payment on the loan in the April and I ended the relationship in the May. But there I was, pregnant, single and scared. "I didn't choose this!"

The scariness didn't last long, though. Being pregnant was the most amazing experience of my life. I was lucky and things went really well, but I did start to suffer with severe back pain, as a result of the cliff rescue. My baby was also a breech birth and had to come out of the emergency hatch. He was a bit yellow, but other than that everything was good. I found a house close to my parents' house and was posted to a naval base within cycling distance of home. Mum looked after my son, Luke, which was great, but my back was causing more and more problems. In the end, I was forced to leave the WRNS as I was no longer physically fit enough for the job. So, at the age of twenty-seven, my career, and whole way of life, was over.

I didn't choose to be a civilian – it was forced upon me and I wasn't ready for it! I didn't understand how it worked and I hated it. I was born into the military. I had no idea how to be anything other than a member of the armed forces.

What I didn't know was that life was changing for a reason. When I was pregnant, I had talked with Mum about how I couldn't cope with a child with a disability. I wasn't up to the task. Fortunately, Luke was the perfect baby. He sat in his pram all day quietly and slept through the night; maybe I was a fabulous mum. But, at play school, Luke couldn't cope with the lack of familiarity and routine. He had massive tantrums and would swipe everything off the tables. He didn't interact with other children and seemed withdrawn. Finally, at four years old, he was diagnosed as autistic. Here I was, the girl who couldn't cope with a disabled child, with a son with special needs. I DIDN'T CHOOSE THIS!

It turns out, though, I was a fantastic mum and advocate for my son. Lots of people get involved in your life when you have a child with extra needs. Mainly, it's to tell you that your child doesn't meet their criteria and so won't receive any support. I became THAT mum. The one who tells these specialists that, actually, they do need to be involved and if they don't sort their… well, you get the message. My military training in resilience and persistence was definitely put to good use. I may not have chosen this role, but I was good at it and I wasn't going to let my little dude down. I had to change my life. Again! But the teeny tiny steps of progress Luke was making made the changes so worthwhile.

I found a job in a GP surgery, as a receptionist and then later as a phlebotomist. It was here that I experienced the worst bullying of my life. One of the doctors had taken a dislike to me and made my life hell. My mental health took a massive nosedive, I was diagnosed with depression and had to leave. I found other roles and loved the work, but struggled with relationships with co-workers. My trust had been eroded and I didn't want to get close to anyone.

Dad came home one day and told us that he had been recalled to the Royal Navy, having completed his service two years earlier, to take a job in Belgium. In order for Luke and I not to be left alone in the UK, he suggested that we go with them. I would have to home educate Luke and rent out my home, but that was fine. After doing a bit of homework into finances, I agreed to go, but there was a niggle in the back of my mind, telling me to stay in the UK. I should have listened! It turns out that I am a terrible teacher! I don't have the patience for it. Luke and I struggled so much and my relationship with my mum took a hit. We just couldn't live together harmoniously. I had lost my identity, being Luke's mum or Keven/Stephanie's daughter. I was no longer Tracey and I was in a really bad way.

That's where the lorry came in. You know. The one that was in front of my car. The one that I had to decide if I wanted to drive into. The thing is, Luke was sitting in the seat next to me. In my mind I could hear those words: "I didn't choose this." Only, I was choosing. I was choosing whether to end Luke's life as well as mine and I couldn't do that to him. He didn't know it, but Luke saved my life that day. If he hadn't been with me, I don't think I would have turned the car.

I knew I had to make some changes and so came back to the UK but continued to teach Luke. I started a counselling course in an attempt to heal myself. It really helped me to see where my focus was and where things had to change. My mental health improved, and I became stronger. Being out of the rat race and spending time at home with just Luke was very healing. I started volunteering with a military charity and met some amazing people. My life started to turn around. Luke successfully transitioned into a mainstream senior school and, in order to stop myself slipping back into a feeling of irrelevance, I took on a volunteer management role within SSAFA, the armed forces charity. Life was better but my health was struggling. I was diagnosed with fibromyalgia, chronic fatigue and anxiety. So, the physically fit, active girl had become an unfit, overweight disabled woman. I didn't choose that!

At around this time, a friend told me about some products his wife was selling that might be able to help with my symptoms. He was right! They were life changing. I signed up to the business, just to get my products at a discount. I wasn't brave enough to build a business. Or was I? If I had learnt anything over the past few years, it was that I had an inner strength. For a while, I had needed to stay at home with Luke, but he was at school now so didn't need me quite so much. I had started a degree with the Open University and had my SSAFA role, but I had pockets of time that I could use to build this business. So that is what I did.

It was slow going. I didn't change from a hermit to a femalepreneur overnight. It took a lot of self-work and mindset shifting. But, over time, I started to realise that the Universe had huge things in store for me. All of those times when I complained about not having chosen my path were times when the Universe was testing to see if I was ready for the next step in my journey. I needed to know more about myself, to have faith in my abilities to advocate for those not able to advocate for themselves. If my health hadn't deteriorated, I would never have left my corporate role. If Luke hadn't been diagnosed with autism, I would never have known how good I was at fighting for others and would never have had the opportunity to work with SSAFA – and would certainly have never taken on a management position. As for starting my own business, never in a million years would I have believed I could do that!

Now Aloe Energetix Health and Wellness allows me to help others improve their health holistically. That was always my aim, but it had a side effect, as I can also help them in a financial way too. I show people how to rise up from the mediocrity of their own lives, to achieve health, wealth and abundance. I show them how to make small changes in order for the Universe to make the big changes.

All of the stresses and worries of my life have changed me and made me into the person I am today. So, my message to those of you stuck in a situation you didn't choose is that this will pass. The Universe has your back. If you put the work in and keep making those small, positive changes, amazing things will happen.

The Universe knows its business. I didn't know that I wanted to move to Cumbria, to be close to my beloved Lake District, but the Universe knew. When I started with my company, I went on a training course and talked about goal setting. I thought it was all a bit pink and fluffy, which is something I certainly am not. But, we were told to write what we really wanted and what we would work hard to achieve. As ex-military, I work hard, no matter what, so no board with pictures on was going to make me work harder. But I dutifully drew a Georgian style house with a long drive and a double garage. It had a roundabout in the front garden and was far too big for Luke and me. I set a date for moving as June 2020.

Over the next few years, I built my business, took on amazing fundraising challenges and was diagnosed with, and beat, cancer. My little light kept shining. I just had a feeling that life was only going to get better.

Eighteen months ago, I attended an SSAFA conference. A man stood up and started to talk about SSAFA in Cumbria. Oh boy, did the Universe give me a kick. I started shaking, having massive palpitations and tears were rolling down my cheeks.

I CHOOSE THAT!

In June 2020 I moved out of my old home and now live in a ridiculously large Georgian house, in Cumbria, with a double garage and a roundabout in the front garden. (It is actually a fountain with walkways round it.) It is the house in the picture I drew four years ago. The Universe knew before I did, and it moved mountains so that I could achieve the dream.

So have faith, keep fighting and a way will open up for you.

★★★

You can find Tracey Here:

www.facebook.com/aloeenergetix

# MY WHIRL OF A ROLLER COASTER RIDE TOWARDS AND INTO THE UNIVERSE!

## Tiarna Ellen Kearns McVerry

*First of all, I would like to tribute this chapter to my amazing mum. Although we do fight like cat and dog a lot of the time, she is my best friend and my absolute rock. Mum is the main reason I am going so good now and the reason for my strength.*

I will be writing about my BPD journey and different events that have brought me into network marketing. I am going to talk about how I got started, most of the things that happened, how I got to where I am now, and some more about what I am doing now and wish to continue with.

I think my journey will have an impact on each reader differently. Everyone at some point in life has been bullied or been the bully – and both of these roles happen for different reasons. Bullying is never okay or 'right' – it's about looking at ourselves and our lives and working on evolving from the inside out.

My emotions now are released through tears, mainly. I would tend to shake, sweat, feel or be sick, but the actual best release for me is tears. I always feel silly and, at times, judged for crying, but it's just my way of letting my emotions out.

It all started, for me, in my early teens.

I started feeling extremely anxious and moody, even more in the last year of primary school.

I always had hospital appointments and a bit of physiotherapy for the physical problems with my legs and feet. Therefore, aside from faking sickness to get out of school, I made any excuse to stay home after appointments also.

When it came to secondary school, things only got worse.

I didn't do too well on the entrance examination. Therefore, based on this, I was placed in a special needs class. This caused uproar with my parents. Everyone knew I was so much better than this. I could DO better.

I was picked on a lot in this group. If it wasn't girls whispering my name to joke around and annoy me, it was writing on the toilet doors, teasing or making fun – it was jealousy when I was praised for my efforts in schoolwork.

I did have a couple of friends in this group, but there was still always a put down.

School life got so bad with these people. During lunchtime one day, as my 'friends' sat with their backs to me, I attempted an overdose. There were loads of people around me and I felt alone. More to the point, no one even noticed what I was doing.

Luckily, I did not have enough tablets to do any

damage. I started to feel extremely sick, so I told a friend in the next class what I had done. I was taken out of school straight away and straight into my doctor's.

I had a couple of days off school while the situation was sorted, and I recovered.

It was around this time dissociation started. That very first time was terrifying. I didn't know who or where I was, noises and voices were so much louder than reality, and everything was closing in around me. All I can remember doing was telling my own head what my own name was and where I lived, along with the directions to my home. I did not actually realise that what I had just done was, in fact, a grounding technique.

This dissociation thing happened loads after this first time and it was ALWAYS terrifying. It still often happens now. However, I can ground myself, as scary as it is.

Around this time, I was put on antidepressants and referred for counselling. I was then referred on to hospital and seen by a psychologist, which went on for several sessions until I was transferred to a psychiatrist for a longer-term treatment plan.

Things seemed to go from bad to worse then.

All the suffering in my own head was bringing out so many moods. I was not a nice person and I was extremely hard to live with. So, my mother ended up asking me to pack my stuff and leave home.

I lived with my grandmother for several months, and then moved into my first flat. I was in a relationship at this time and, although it was not the healthiest, he did visit and stayed with me a couple of nights each week.

This flat I lived in was not close to my family or friends. I ended up hating the flat and hating the area even more. As well as this, when I was ill, my family had to drive to me, or I had to get lifts or taxis to get to them. It was not practical.

Soon, my (at the time) boyfriend and I got a house together. It was great for a while and then the cracks started to show. We both had problems that needed fixing and things started to fall apart. When the relationship finally ended, I broke. Although it wasn't love, and the relationship was unhealthy, my BPD traits kicked in: I feared being alone and being thought badly of.

I stayed single then for two years.

I went to appointments, support groups, mental health services and I had several key workers at different times.

I never settled in support groups – they were just not for me.

Appointments did help but key workers changed so often that I was left confused and anxious.

After the two years of being alone, I wanted a new relationship – and I found one. It turned out to be so much worse than my last one. I didn't clean my house, I never had any money, I started to lose my friends, but I also started drinking loads more than normal.

One night I had a drink with two friends. I had vodka, not realising how ill I was, and I attempted to self-harm, but turned on my friends. It could have ended much worse than it did. However, my mum was called, and she got things settled. The next morning the doctor confirmed I had alcohol psychosis. I was TERRIFIED and extremely embarrassed.

Having this unhealthy relationship, and then this episode of psychosis, dissociating often and the way I generally felt within myself was draining and extremely frustrating.

I was losing myself; I was blamed for everything. Everything was my fault and even my professional health services also got blame.

This relationship was majorly holding me back from everything. From living, growing, evolving, recovering, improving, developing – literally everything. And, at this time, for a long while, I was the only one who could not see any of this.

The relationship after this one was good. There were no faults for four months straight, then he sent me a message to end things as he needed to recover from an unexpected illness. But I had seen through social media that he was chatting up others. So, head in a spiral again: was I not good enough?

Pretty much over the years, the smallest, silliest things have annoyed me, or affected me in some way. Because my diagnosis is pretty much based on intense, unstable emotions – especially in relationships – a small argument could be massive in my mind, and happiness or excitement could be euphoric.

Anxiety would be one trait. However, generally, the main trait would be anger. I was riddled with anger and frustration in younger years.

The diagnosis has several different names, the most

common being Borderline Personality Disorder, but it's mostly known as Emotional Unstable Personality Disorder.

Other traits of this disorder alongside anger and anxiety would be depression, self-image and identity issues, unstable moods and relationships, impulsive actions and the dissociative spells. All me, but at this point in life, different traits at different times, for different reasons. And, at times, with the wrong people.

Due to research, studying, appointments and years of suffering and experiences, I have learned I need to be around positive, happy people, learn from my mistakes and move on. Self-help, self-care, self-love are essential, and positivity is key!

Several years ago, a relative from overseas saw my negativity on social media and, being in network marketing at this time, she aimed to help me get involved to grow positivity, both on and offline.

I did get a few sales and my confidence started to grow, until I got my first team member. I gave her the same advice that my relative had given her, but the girl turned on me and a whole situation started. I was asked, or more so advised, to step back and take some time out, but being so close to a promotion, I felt as though I was being held back, so then things got so much worse.

After this situation, I tried two other different companies. One I absolutely LOVED, and the other one had quite a bit of bullying and jealousy within the team, which won't go very far with anyone! Two of those companies I tried were aiming to empower women, and to me, this is not what those teams were about.

I kept trying and working, planning, writing, supporting and looking out for something that was more suited to me. All I knew by this point was that I wanted to help and support others.

There have been times I slacked a lot. This was usually due to physical pain, sickness, lack of sleep and mental health issues.

I have always been a writer.

I remember writing a poem at a young age, which blew my mother's mind! I did FOLDERS of writing for studies and then started to write diaries and journals, which progressed to putting my notes together and publishing my own recovery journey!

I joined, again, a company I was previously with, but then decided upon more, with the idea of relating each to my help and support work.

So now I had been setting up my five online businesses, working on continuing as an author, working on supporting people and setting up more in regard to support work.

Now these online businesses have decreased to three, and I am focusing more on self-development and coursework!

I also have a lot of training materials with these two amazing girls, which really helps with so much to reflect on!

Going back to my diagnosis, in regard to everything I am doing now, it all helps to set goals, plan things out, get into mindset and spiritual work, healings and meditations.

I do know people have said, and I have caught out some people saying, or mentioning in conversations that I'm 'not all there', 'crazy', 'attention seeking', 'making excuses', and other stuff similar.

Believe me, I have a disorder, yes, I am borderline, yes, but I am more normal than a load of others out there. Yes, I can be too open sometimes, kind of outspoken, and sometimes childlike for a twenty-nine year old, but I am me. I am my own normal, and I am learning slowly that I do not need to 'fit in', and I KNOW I wasn't born to fit in, as such, either.

Growing up, I was not spiritual. I took an interest in psychic readings around three, maybe four years ago, but before this, I joined a local prayer group specifically to get out to meet people and begin to socialise more, and I then became intrigued in the meanings behind this group. I did drop out a couple of times with health reasons and, in the end, decided not to go back. However, intrigued as I am into spiritual development now, I have my own research, work, social media, and amazing people to learn from.

I do believe this group was brought to me for a reason and now I am on a journey of self-discovery, influence, spirituality and gratitude.

Part of my reason for leaving the group, apart from illness, was because I wanted to focus on my work and growing with my plans.

My three online businesses are a lot of work, admittedly, but it does not stop there…

I have loads of training work with the girls, my

upcoming online support services and also my online studies. My studies include counselling, CBT, coaching, mindfulness and meditation, and healing work, as well as studying crystals and the power of the moon.

All of my work together aims to help and support people in different ways.

I also have my own book published, sharing my mental health journey to give others some hope in recovery, and in life. So, I am therefore, a newly published author.

I am slowly becoming more successful, which was a goal for 2020, and I have the motivation now to grow this success and to help others to become more successful also.

Recently, with my mental health, I became inactive in two of my businesses. However, I have started some intense therapy, which I know I need, and this is a positive for me as it gives me more time to plan business work and decide where to REALLY put my full focus from here!

I can have my thinking time now, on which businesses would be of more benefit, and suit me more, and in relation to other work, as I aim to relate all towards helping and supporting other people.

I can then rejoin and continue with a clearer mind and take this time to grow and work on myself, which if someone had suggested this option to me around five or so years ago, I would have broken down!

I am more accepting now of the place I'm at, and I know exactly what needs to be done. The best thing I have done EVER is become a femalepreneur – and I will only grow bigger, better and stronger.

I adore these two girls, and all the work they do. I am extremely appreciative towards them, both JoJo and Tasha, I will be forever grateful for them, and I absolutely adore them!

★★★

You can find Tiara here:

www.facebook.com/tiarna.e.kearn
www.instagram.com/tiarnakearns
www.facebook.com/tribewithtia

# BELIEVE YOU DESERVE IT AND THE UNIVERSE WILL SERVE IT

## Rachel Petford

*I dedicate this chapter to my husband, thank you for always believing in me, even when I couldn't believe in myself.*

Standing there in the busy high street, the sun beaming down on my face warming my cheeks, the smell of summer was in the air. I could hear laughter all around me but inside I was broken, I just wanted to scream. I was so tired of putting on a mask to the world, pretending to be okay. The seven-year volatile relationship I was in had stripped me of my identity; who even was I anymore? I knew in that moment enough was enough, I had to get out.

But there was one problem, who do I turn to, who could I ask for help?! My family had put up with me stealing, lying and taking drugs. My friends had had enough of me staying with someone who abused me. I felt lost and alone, who would want to help me?! After all, I deserved this, I rebelled against my family!

You see, I was a church girl, from the age of one I had

been going to church. My whole life had evolved around the church. Everything my family had taught me, I had disregarded, and completely gone against them and God.

Why should anyone help me now? Maybe I didn't deserve a better life! What if all this was punishment, punishment for all the defiant things I had done to my parents. The guilt consumed me, eating away at my very being. No matter how hard I tried, I couldn't shake off the guilt. Everything around me felt dark. How was I ever going to get out of this?! But I knew I owed it to myself to pick myself up and start again, no matter what it took; I couldn't feel this way anymore. And in that moment, I looked up at him and said, "I am not doing this anymore." And I walked away, keeping my eyes forward, fixated on the path ahead.

I am not about to tell you my life miraculously turned around, but I can tell you that from that moment on things began to change. Obviously, the pain, the hurt that was caused had to come out. I spent days crying into a pillow with a gut-wrenching feeling deep in the pit of my stomach. I had to take time to heal, but slowly I began to shake off the guilt. What had happened to me wasn't my fault. I had made those choices in my life and now I had another choice to make, do I wallow here on my bed or do I get up and start living?

I made a conscious decision to look at everything around me differently. The grass was now green again and the sky was blue. Oh, how I had missed so much. Spending time with friends and family became more natural again. The guilt and embarrassment was slowly shifting, being replaced with laughter; you know, the one where you laugh so much that no sound comes out. I began to shine again. You never really understand whilst you are in that deep dark hole just how much it steals your sunshine, until you see friends again and they say how happy you look. And you feel it, you really do. A smile that covers your whole face is back again. I was back, back to feeling like me.

Having a broken heart can still make you feel damaged, and you question if you will ever find love, the real love, love that makes you feel safe and warm. You can go round in circles, could you even trust anyone, would you get hurt again? Your mind plays awful tricks on you, trying to protect you from more pain. I honestly didn't think I could trust anyone, but oh how wrong was I.

It was a year on from my breakup, and I was feeling quite good about myself. I was sitting down on the beach, the waves crashing in the distance, seagulls flying overhead. I could feel the sand between my toes. When, all of a sudden, out of nowhere, there stands a 6ft 1 handsome, well-built guy wearing black sunglasses and little shorts. From then on, I knew I was in trouble.

What a different relationship this was. I had been used to feeling on edge, not knowing what was going to happen next. But Ryan was so loving and caring, he made me feel safe. The problem was, I was conditioned to expect it all to come crashing down. Self-sabotage was now my middle name. That feeling of 'did I deserve this' crept back into my head. I constantly waited for something to happen that would ruin it. I was so terrified of losing it all. So, there I was, losing myself again.

Ryan had so much confidence, especially for a twenty-two year old. I couldn't believe he was so young. He was so wise and driven. I hadn't been around anyone like this for a long time. He knew what he wanted and wasn't afraid about going and getting it. This scared me, I wasn't like that, I had become a person who played it safe. What could he see in me, I didn't have anything to offer him? I was so afraid to show him my wounds that I put my mask back on, brushing off any feelings that would come up. 'Just get on with it,' I would often tell myself. 'No one wants to hear your problems! Don't bring anyone else down!' If you do this often enough, you soon forget who you are, what your passions are, what you want to do in your lifetime. Don't get me wrong, I mean, he made me happy, oh so happy. He showed me how to be confident again, I experienced love, true love for the first time and it was incredible, but I wasn't doing anything for me. And don't forget I had spent seven years previously hiding away, not being able to communicate properly with anyone. It wasn't my natural instinct to put myself first, my needs, my desires. I had built up a wall in which I could help others and make sure they had everything, but I couldn't express my own feelings. I sat back and watched Ryan grow and progress in the gym we had opened, supporting him in any way I could; after all, he had literally saved me.

We were now at that stage in a relationship when you start to talk about having children. This was it, my time.

I had always wanted to be a mum, coming from a large family, being the oldest of five children. Having my own one day truly gave me that spark. You start trying and it's all exciting at first, then one year goes by, then two, then three. Okay, is this because of my past again? Am I being punished?! Do I not deserve to have my own children?! I struggled to understand. Four years went by. The heartache was unbearable. The endless scan pictures from friends each year with those words I am longing to say: 'I am pregnant'. Please do not get me wrong, I was always so happy for my friends. They deserved to have children. But was it just me who didn't deserve them?

It doesn't matter how many masks you put on, it doesn't change who you are underneath, and for me, that was someone who in my teens had made some mistakes but was now punishing myself for them, believing in a silly lie that I didn't deserve true happiness. I couldn't really tell anyone how I was feeling, I was so afraid to break down and crack that mask. People weren't used to me crying about anything. I guess I felt like I was being weak if I let it affect me.

In spite of my feelings that I was being punished and didn't deserve true happiness, the universe, the creator had my back. Randomly, I got tagged in a post for a competition, the winnings being an advent calendar full of perfumes. It was free and I absolutely love perfume, so I thought 'why not, no harm in sharing a post'. To my surprise, I actually won the competition, totally shocked but excited to receive my winnings. What a result, twenty-three designer-inspired perfumes and a full size

THE ELEVATION OF THE *Femalepreneur*

one. My obsession grew, so much so that I decided to join the company. At the beginning, it was just to get myself more of a discount on my ever-growing perfume collection, but then it became more. People wanted to join my team, my sales were increasing weekly, and I was really enjoying it. Without realising it, I was doing something for me. Something I could get my teeth into that wasn't attached to anyone else. This was giving me focus and purpose and helping me to forget about our fertility journey. But was it just another mask I could put on?!

It was 2020 and, wow, hearing on the news that there was a deadly virus and we would have to shut our gym was terrifying and so daunting; what was going to happen?!

I knew I would have to do something to earn more money and wasn't I grateful that I had started my NWM business in December the previous year. It was all hands on deck, I was going to work as hard as I could to really build up this business. My upline was incredible, the support offered to me was second to none. She really believed in me. I couldn't believe how much my confidence had grown in such a short space of time. I was helping to do training videos to the wider team and supporting and encouraging so many different ladies. I was buzzing, the excitement to work every day was so addictive. The fire in my belly was back. I was passionate again and everyone could see it. You know when you start talking to people about what you are doing, and you light up. The joy when I would talk about the products, about my team, about all the inspiring women I got to be around. How this company was literally transforming my life. From the pit of despair, out of the mud and mire, my feet were now on solid ground being guided as I walked this journey. My soul ignited, thinking about how different I had become and how grateful I was for this opportunity. Honestly, if you had told me in 2019 that I would be doing network marketing and have my own team to lead, I would have laughed. There was no way I would have had the confidence to do sales, let alone show a team of women how to do it as well. But here I was, owning it and loving every second.

I wouldn't have thought things could get any better than this. My team was over 100 ladies, I had hit the top of the comp plan and then hit the leadership status of Pearl. I couldn't believe how much money I was making from a little perfume obsession. But my story does get better, it wasn't all about the money for me. It was about doing something for myself and I was finally feeling like I had a purpose, finally at the age of thirty-six I had stepped out on my own and embraced who I truly was. A confident, creative, intelligent woman, capable of anything that I put my mind to.

Being introduced to the Femalepreneur Academy was the ultimate game changer for me. I remember watching a video of Natasha and just thinking, 'Okay, you speak my language, I want to know more.' I don't know if you have ever experienced synchronicity before, where you were either talking or thinking about something then you see it everywhere. Well, this kept happening with the Femalepreneurs' content. That fire in my belly was burning and my heart was feeling full. I knew I was exactly where I was supposed to be. I was beginning to believe I deserved all this and more. All my worries were slowly drifting away, the foggy brain had now become clear and free, ready to learn more and find out more about what I was truly capable of.

There I was after the moon manifesting course thinking, 'What's next?' Usually, the doubt would creep in, I would start wondering if I deserved more, was this my limit, but this time I was like 'heck yes, I want more and I'm going to get it'. Different courses started popping up on my phone, so I enrolled. This is something I would not have done before; I wouldn't have had the confidence to put myself out there. The first course, hot stones massage, I passed with a higher distinction. This felt good, so I took another one, Indian head massage, another higher distinction. Who was this person?! The feeling of passing was so satisfying. And, would you believe it, I went on to do meditation and visualisation then reiki. I also enrolled in a hypnotherapy course, reflexology and a life coach and counselling course. It is incredible what happens once you believe you deserve it. Your powers are endless. I don't tell you this to show off, I am telling you this because that once beaten-down, insecure, not worthy, undeserving little girl has transformed into a confident, worthy, loved and all-deserving woman. The cage I had once built around myself had merely been a cocoon. Often people say, 'Would you change anything from your past?' And I would say, 'I wouldn't change a thing because it taught me how to fly.' Life showed me that you can go through a lot of darkness and still become something beautiful.

Life won't always be easy, there will be ups and downs, but just think, I was once a girl who couldn't even make a phone call without sweaty palms and a heartbeat that felt like it would break through my chest. Everyday tasks crippled me and I kept it all inside, just building up the layers, hiding behind so many masks, replacing one thing for another to avoid dealing with my true feelings. Then one day I realised I did deserve to be confident, to have a happy, fulfilling life. To stop believing that my past had defined me and was punishing me.

Our fertility journey is still ongoing but I am at peace with it. I deserve to have children and one day in the not-so-distant future I will have them. I just have to believe it.

Remember, the universe wants you to win. You just have to believe it and success will follow. Trust in yourself and learn to love who you truly are. You are beautiful, for you are fearfully and wonderfully made.

You can find Rachel here:

www.instagram.com/fiercefemaleshearusroar
https://www.facebook.com/FierceFemalesHearUsRoar/

# FALLEN

## Nicky Bright

*This chapter is dedicated to the two wonderful children I
brought into this world, Lewis and Morgan. You always believe
the impossible is possible. I love you always and forever, Mum.*

As a young twenty-one year old, I thought I had the
future mapped out. I would leave high school, go to
college, have a good job and find my future husband. I
had grown up from a working-class family, Dad worked
away from home and Mum managed the family. I was
the eldest of five children, mini mum to my younger
siblings. My memories of my childhood were fun and
exciting. I especially remember Christmases, Easter and
family events. Being part of a large family, I enjoyed
family gatherings with Grandad, head of the family,
"Boss Man". My future was to include one day having
my own family. I visualised two children, the type of
house I would live in, even a little dog. My future had
the same values I had grown up with as a child; love,
trust and loyalty.

Twenty-five years on, I found myself lying in the
dark on the sofa crying, sobbing, questioning what went

wrong. I wanted someone to help me, it felt like the walls were crumbling around me, as if my life was slipping away. I wanted to surrender, but I wouldn't because it was not in me to give up, not in my blueprint, my DNA. I felt overwhelmed, lonely and insecure, needing strength to take away the pain, to make me feel like me again. My mind needed a rest, no medicine or sipping wine would cheer me up!

Spinning through my mind was my life. Everywhere I looked, from my telephone to walking past a shop, memories sparked back up… birthdays, Valentines', anniversaries, Christmas… total torment. What did I do so wrong for my husband to walk out on me and my children with no notice, no plan and no time to prepare? Twenty-five years married to a person I thought I knew better than myself left me broken. How could someone you love leave you in so much pain? How was I going to figure out a plan after my life had just hit the reset button?

It was a sunny spring day. I woke up to a normal family morning, children off to school and work with me preparing to leave for the store, which wasn't far away. I loved my job, retail store manager for menswear, and had been with the company for nine years, climbing the ladder.

I said goodbye to my husband and children, and off to work I went. My life was good; two children, well-paid careers, lovely home, cars, holidays that we all work for. I was having a normal busy day in store, managing staff along with daily trading business. I remember the day well; the store was busy and the telephone kept ringing and ringing. I remember looking around and all the staff were engaged serving customers, including me. The incoming call was on redial. I looked over to see a cashier become available and I heard her greeting the caller: "She's busy at the moment, can I take a message?" I turned, had eye contact with the cashier, and she informed me, "It's an urgent call." I took the call, it was my son, and I asked if it could wait until I arrived home.

What I was about to discover from a phone call was to change my life forever, and would take me to my knees with the biggest fall I have ever taken... "Mum, Dad's having an affair."

I remember standing in the middle of the store on the telephone, questioning what news I had just received. I was left standing frozen in time. I looked around and everyone around me was laughing, joking, smiling, serving customers. I felt I wasn't inside my own body, a sense of free falling.

With just a ten minute journey from store to home, what was I about to discover?

During the short drive home, millions of voices were screaming in my mind. Where was he on the days he stayed away from home? New clothes he had bought, late night trips to the supermarket to leave the house. My gut had been screaming red flags; why didn't I trust my instinct? How had I missed what was going on around me? It was my job to notice my surroundings in store with staff, customers and shoplifters, how had I allowed this to happen?

Why? Because he was my husband, I trusted him. Who was she? Was she someone I knew? How long had it been going on?

We had only just arrived home from a family holiday to New York, were all those happy family pictures now fake? With my manager mind, I even questioned the possibility of my children making a mistake. They were young adults aged sixteen and twenty-one, they must have heard or seen something.

I parked my car on the drive, locked it up and entered the house. I left my briefcase in the same place I leave it every evening after work in the hall.

In the next ten footsteps, I would confront my husband who was home. I walked into the lounge and found him watching TV. I stood opposite him and confronted him with the news the children had given me. "Are you having an affair?" It took no more than a few seconds and he replied YES. I felt numb, in shock, my mind spinning with questions. How was this possible? Why didn't I know? I asked if she loved him. He said yes. Do you love her? I have feelings for her. I didn't cry, I was in shock and worried about what was going through the children's minds. What did the future look like now? How was it going to pan out? Millions of thoughts per second, "fight or flight" kicked in.

I asked him to leave. He packed a small holdall he would normally use for work containing the clothes I bought him, wearing the aftershave I gave him for Christmas, and went to the woman he was having an affair with, an ex-girlfriend from high school.

I didn't eat or sleep that weekend. It was Easter and the weather was beautiful, warm, ideal for a spring BBQ. I had everything planned for the family Easter break; little did I know what was planned for me! I wasted no time. Monday morning I was with my solicitor and filed for a divorce. I was shaking, still in shock. She asked if I needed more time. I said NO, he had broken my values – trust, loyalty, family and love – and he could never return.

Looking back, I thought the first six weeks was tough, even three months. What I know now was it got harder and harder. I asked my solicitor how long it would take to divorce him. Six months? She replied years. If I knew what I know now I would not have focused on a divorce and instead put all the energy into myself.

Whilst lying in the dark on the sofa, I heard my children enter the hallway. I could hear my daughter speaking. "I'm scared to go in, she may be dead." Using the torch from their mobile phone, they entered the lounge. My son placed his hand over my mouth to confirm I was breathing. It was in this moment I knew I had to take action; it reminded me of being ten years of age and scared to enter a dark room as my grandmother had passed away in my bedroom in my bed. I was scared like my children were feeling. From that moment, a bolt of energy inside me woke me up; you have a job to do, stand up!

I gathered my children, and we hugged and cried together. I promised them I would find a solution to save our home and rebuild what was destroyed. The words "are you having an affair" haunted me over the next twelve months. Little did I know, more bad news was about to be delivered to me, further dragging me down to my knees, losing my hair, home and finally my job.

The only way to describe how I felt at the time was a feeling of loss, as if my husband had died and with it my life too. I didn't know, but at the time, I was grieving for my life, the only life I had known for twenty-five years. The place I called home, the place I felt safe with the people I loved.

The beach became my safe place, the place I felt happy and had many mindful discussions with myself, planning my future.

I finished work early one summer evening and decided to take the dogs for a walk. I passed the village pub where I had sat hundreds of times over the years with family and friends. I could see my husband sitting with our children having lunch. I looked on whilst crying, thinking I should be there, why wasn't I there? They are my family, what did I do that was so wrong? Why me? Twenty-five years together, we were best friends, why would my best friend and the person I loved want to do this to me, knowing it would destroy me? I started to blame myself and question: was I not pretty enough for him anymore? Was I too old now? I kept asking myself the same questions over and over, tormenting myself.

The first three months, I cried every day. I looked in the mirror and the person looking back at me wasn't the confident lady I recognised. Where was she? I needed her now more than ever, she would know what to do, she is good at resolving problems. I had to find myself again, the younger girl who dreamt, had fun and was always happy. I needed her back in my life to hold my hand and take me into my future.

Sitting on my bed became the place I spent most of my life for the next three years, repairing and licking my wounds. I walked around my home, entering each room, removing memories that kept giving me pain. At first, I moved them into the spare room and, with time, I was able to part with them. Picking up items as I entered each room on a time zone into my past, I picked up gifts the children had bought me for Mother's Day, my favourite jewellery my husband had given me, packing them away into boxes, along with my engagement and wedding ring. Looking at family photo albums of my babies and all the items I had saved one day for my grandchildren, the same question would return into my mind: "WHY?"

I could feel the energy of my children, younger, running around screaming and laughing inside the four walls. As I left each room, I thanked the house for the beautiful memories I would take with me, leaving only the loving energy behind.

Over the years ahead, I would fight legal battles with my husband. I looked across the courtroom to a man I once loved, thinking, 'I would never have done this to you or our family.' There we were in a courtroom fighting over assets and sofas.

The pressure of selling the family home and divorce meant I finally lost my job. The job I loved; it was my baby, along with the team I had grown. The writing was on the wall; I knew my personal life was affecting my work. I lost focus; I wasn't the person I had been anymore. I wasn't happy, I was sad and lost. I was living in fear of the unknown future.

I received the news via my solicitor that the bank was taking the house from us. With no time to prepare or plan, I told the children to pack small bags, leaving everything behind, including the food in the fridge, until I could return and pack. It felt like my life was getting worse not better. With no job, yet another bombshell was awaiting me.

Sitting on my bed, the place that had become my safe place, my girl cave, I looked at my laptop, picked it up and decided to send an email to anyone who worked for the bank. I had to stop the repossession order taking place. I wasn't prepared to lose the only asset I had left. I spent the evening locating as many email addresses as possible and hit send. Every email I sent was returned as rejected, but I didn't give up; the law of averages says one person in 100 will respond, so I didn't give up. I went to bed exhausted, thinking of a plan B. The following day was a Sunday, I opened my emails and there it was at the top of my inbox, one email from a senior manager at the bank saying he would call me in the morning. I remember feeling so happy that someone had heard my voice. The following day was the day my life would change forever! An action plan was put in place and we were okay for now!

What I had learnt from the past four years was that the only person who can save me is me.

If I could go back in time, I wouldn't focus on what I was losing, I would focus on myself, my future, my plans, what a new life would look like. Invest in you, look for new hobbies, sports and a new circle of friends. I have learnt to horse ride, play golf, even clay pigeon shooting. Once you make a list of all the wonderful things you missed out on, or simply just didn't have the time to do, take the action and amazing things happen.

Once I started to let go of the past twenty-five years because it wasn't going to serve me in my future, the happier I became. A "transition of change", life was different now, it was my awakening from falling. I felt like a caterpillar whose life was to crawl around but one day awakened into a new life feeling youthful, beautiful and free to fly anywhere in the world… it's amazing when the butterfly flies away, they forget they used to crawl in their past life.

I started to visualise the future, a future of happiness and falling in love, feeling safe, secure, starting my own business, and NickyBright.com was born.

The time had come, my beautiful home had sold and it was time for me to leave and for another family to enjoy it. I left with only a suitcase, everything I once cherished sold and stayed inside.

I locked up and walked away, never to look back, taking only the memories I made with me, as well as the two beautiful children I brought into this world to join me on my new adventure.

The best lesson I learnt in life has come from the worst feeling I ever felt in life, how to pick myself up from falling.

★★★

You can find Nicky here:

Twitter.com/nickybrighthols
Instagram.com/nickybrightholidays
https://www.facebook.com/Nicky.J.Bright

# FROM FEAR TO FREEDOM

## Claire Garbett

*In this chapter, I'm going to be sharing one thing that sets you free and helps you create a life your soul already knows you are worthy of…*

*This is dedicated to everyone out there who, when growing up, felt trapped in fear inside the one place they should feel the safest. I write this to let you know you have the choice to set yourself free, that you are good enough, worthy enough… and don't ever let your past define or limit who you are or what you were brought here to create.*

I was once asked, 'What's the first fairy tale or children's story that comes to your mind?'

'Three Little Pigs.'

As the teacher was analysing each story that came up for others in the group, my jaw kept dropping lower and lower as I realised my fairy tale was my childhood in a nutshell; constantly moving from home to home, trying to get away from the Big Bad Wolf, my dad! This is where I started on a roller coaster of ups and downs of finding who I truly am. I had to stop relying on pre-

prepared building blocks and learn to build my own for my own safety and stability because I realised the wolf can only be at the door if I allow it to be.

From a young age, I always felt like I was walking on eggshells, always expecting the worst, fuelled with fear, anxiety and panic attacks. Where anything you do is never good enough or you're just a number. Growing up in a violent environment, never knowing when the next kick off is going to happen, or when we must 'flee' to safety was head spinning. Bouncing from safe houses to new homes, from school to school, made it hard to make lasting friendships. I was lucky there were so many of us. I had five sisters and a brother; I was number two!

Here I was at twenty-three years old in my darkest place yet. I'd just gone through a lengthy court case, dragging up the past, my childhood memories, running out of the house, grabbing as many of my siblings as possible. Don't get noticed. Don't get caught in the crossfire. Mopping up the aftermath, watching the ones I love crying due to the pain, anger or frustration of not being able to get out of the situation. My own frustration and anger – why us, what's the point of being here if this is all we get or all we have? The times I've wanted to end my life as I couldn't cope with the one I had (oh my days, I'm so glad now that I didn't go through with it!).

All this while being pregnant with my second child. My pregnancy was focused on keeping him in, of not knowing whether the little one would stay with us. Constantly in and out of hospital, then boom seven weeks early I went into labour just after my days in court... all I thought was that this was my fault because of what we were doing to my dad. What goes around comes around. I take part in him losing his freedom then I have something taken away from me... that's right, isn't it? Isn't that what we're told?

After two weeks in hospital with intermittent labour, my son was born the day before what we called 'D-Day' – my dad's reckoning... would we be rid of the constant fear and black cloud over us or would it continue? Three weeks of intensive care for my son and healing for me, I felt I was getting lower in my spirits, the struggle of the court case that had lasted a year, my traumatic pregnancy and birth, constantly reliving the feelings of not being good enough, no self-worth, reliving the traumas of not only the violence in the home as a child but the drug-induced rape I endured at sixteen years old. Going into the past brought everything up; all I could think was that I was always going to have shit happen to me! Depression hit me hard, but little did I know it was going to be the making of me; when you are breaking down, you are about to break through...

After being told he'd got fifteen years in prison, it hit me, I had a CHOICE... Do I continue to live the victim role and be in constant fear, or am I going to let this shit go and find the real me, my happiness, my soul purpose?

Hell yeah! My past will not define me!

So, I joined a personal development course, built up the courage to go to college and volunteer in my daughter's primary school, which led me to become a full time TA. Never in a month of Sundays did I think I was good enough to work in a school! I had no GCSEs, at sixteen years old it was about survival for me, not education! It was 'get a job or you're on the streets' (which is where I met my hubby… in one of the many factories I worked in). My role in the school changed and evolved during my twelve years there. I became a learning mentor, which opened my eyes to how much trauma I had in common with these kids. I empathised with them. I knew what they meant when they said, 'it's normal, it's okay'. I recognised the fear of getting their parents into trouble if they spoke to anyone. It helped me to see my childhood in a different light, from different points of views. While at college, I trained in massage, reflexology, etc. I actually found something I enjoyed doing and I felt I was good at it, something that felt like my calling. I knew after a year or so that I wanted to run my own business as a holistic therapist. I introduced a holistic approach in school, bringing in techniques I was learning, like meditation, crystals, MISP and Relax Kids, and it was making such a difference with the kids and myself. But I felt like I was still missing something. I kept going up and down with my emotions, I felt like every time I took a step forward within myself, I then got thrown back again. Every year, I felt I needed more input all the time – always a learner, never a doer. It was, 'I just need to do one more course', I never thought I was good enough, I judged myself all the time and expected others to do the same! I was working my ass off with two jobs, training, looking after my family and I just didn't have the confidence to make a decision, didn't believe in myself that I could actually make my business work; I was stuck in the lack mentality!

I was drawn to Energy Healing and decided I needed this to let go of past emotional ties. Oh my days, once I was initiated, my world was turned upside down and back again, but this time with a different perspective. I kicked some old beliefs out and, after a year within this new energy, I sold my house and moved to a small village. I never thought I'd be able to move far from my siblings as I always felt I needed to be close – just in case – but that was the fear mentality!

I was linking with more like-minded 'woo woo' people! I felt I was getting close to finding me but there was just something niggling at the back of my mind. Then boom! A family fall out. My gut kept telling me to bring myself away and at that time I was learning to trust my instincts. Coming away from my siblings was the hardest thing I've ever done. They were the people I went to when I needed help, support, guidance. They were my safety net. We love each other dearly and would do anything for each other. But I felt constrained, like there would be nothing more than the family unit. We had built a fortress around us throughout our lives. But our fortress had become a suffocating embrace. I needed space to think for myself, to set new boundaries. I wanted to push those boundaries to see how far I could actually go. I did struggle with this but kept working with the energies, working on myself and trusting it was the right decision, and wowsers, it really was. I started listening to my own intuition and doing what was right for me.

Putting me first for the first time in my life, caring about myself and my feelings instead of everyone else's. Don't get me wrong, I didn't become selfish, I always took others' feelings into consideration, but did what was right for me at that time. I found this hard at times, and had to consciously keep asking myself, 'Is this okay with you, is it what will make you happy?' I then took a leap of faith and handed in my notice at school. I just kept thinking I've gone mad, what if it doesn't work? I can't go back; I'd be a failure! This is when I had to start asking for help. My mindset at the time always said, 'Don't ask for help as it's a sign of weakness.' DUH, what an idiot! Looking back, I should have known better, as the fundamental rule working with young children was that you should never feel bad or ashamed about asking for help. So, I started picking my clients' brains – my 'Soul Clients' as I now know them. Each and every one of them had skills of their own that helped me each step of the way, whether it be in advertising, marketing, accounting or just giving me that love and boost of confidence. It's amazing what happens when you choose to be around people that lift your spirit. The opportunities are endless!

I started to read up on manifesting and the Law of Attraction. Oh my days, it's fricking bonkers how this stuff works… you ask and you receive. At first, I thought, 'Yep, Claire, you're definitely losing the plot!' Standing in the middle of the room talking out loud to the universe, even the hubby who went along with everything else started to look at me as if to say, 'Do I need to call in the men with the white coats?!' But things were actually dropping into place! The more I believed and asked, the more my business was building. And so were my friendships, beliefs, trust in others and myself. I was having revelation after revelation and still am to this day. Every day is a school day, I'm learning more about the world around me and more importantly the 'being' within me! The more I listened and trusted my intuition, the more things fell into place, there was a flow. The more I did meditations, energy healing and working within, the more I became my true self. Within my meditations, I started to get clarity and clear visions of what I should be doing. Just so you know, working on yourself isn't always being on a high, you do get those knocks that come out of nowhere and, yep, I'd just hit another block. I knew I was having big shifts, changing my mindset, using all the tools I'd been given, etc., but I felt like I was stuck again. Then it hit me while on a shamanic journey… I needed to forgive. I thought, 'Not a chance am I saying "it's okay" to those people that have hurt or caused me pain.' It just brought back the anger and fear – seriously, how are you supposed to forgive those that cause you so much harm, whether that be physically, mentally or emotionally?

I had to trust that the universe had my back!

I realised, forgiving didn't mean I had to excuse people for the hurt and pain I'd endured or that I had to make up with them or have them in my life. The forgiveness was for ME. For ME to find peace. For ME to find hope. For ME to let go of the emotional ties of anger and being in the victim role; it didn't bother or affect them at all. It only hurt ME, and *I* was stopping ME from moving forward in all aspects of my life, including my business!

I truly believe that finding forgiveness releases you from so many restraints in life, not just mentally, but physically and spiritually too. It's led me to a new type of energy work, it's given me a deeper understanding of my own power within, a new way of healing myself and others, which in turn has boosted my business, pushing my fast forward button for a deeper connection with spirit. I am now working online linking with other like-minded people who I would never have met as I'd never have had the courage to step out of my comfort zone before. It has freed me to do what I was meant to do. To be in alignment with my soul purpose. To help others on their path and find their light within, so they can find what's true for them and in turn help the next person and so on!

Don't get me wrong, it's not been easy, it takes commitment and, for me, meditation, energy work, spiritual connection and lots of trust… but it ain't half worth it!

When I look back now, I was the girl trapped in FEAR. I didn't believe I was good enough or clever enough, I had no value or self-worth. I spent so much time trying to hide from who I truly was, trying to fit in, trying to be what everyone else wanted me to be; so, all my life, I have held back from my truth, from speaking my truth, allowing others to make me feel as if my thoughts and feelings are not important, all because I believed in fear, and I held anger for past situations and people. I lived in the victim mentality. I was my own worst enemy, I definitely held myself and my business back!

So, for those that are still here reading my story, in my opinion the one thing that truly sets you free is 'forgiveness'. Don't get wrapped up in the wrong done to you in the past, as you miss the present, the now, the amazing people, opportunities and places that surround you now!

Go ahead, start your journey, find forgiveness, find your true self, set yourself free from fear. Find what makes your heart shine and in doing so lead the life that you love!!

★★★

You can find Claire here:

https://www.facebook.com/theknottedtree/
https://www.instagram.com/the_knotted_tree/

# IT'S NEVER TOO LATE TO
# FOLLOW YOUR DREAMS

## *Sarah Wallace*

*This chapter is dedicated to my darling mum, who often said these wise words to me, 'Sarah, life is not a dress rehearsal.' To my family who are without doubt my raison d'etre. And to my husband, Albert, who has patiently stood by my side while I got there and finally allowed me to believe in me. I love you all, thank you.*

As I lifted my head from the toilet bowl and wiped the vomit from around my face, I looked into the mirror with despair at my red face and swollen, streaming eyes and vowed to myself, this would be the last time…

I started having self-image and body issues from the age of about fourteen and this developed into full-blown bulimia by the age of sixteen. When it came to the attention of my family and became apparent that I had a real problem, my mother took me to the doctor, and I was referred to an eating disorder specialist, who I subsequently saw once a week for ten weeks. The therapist was a young, attractive woman, who I immediately liked and built a rapport with and, wanting to be a good student for her, I did well and succeeded in getting a handle on it. This was short-lived, however, because as soon as I stopped seeing her, things deteriorated again.

I didn't have a bad childhood, quite the opposite really. My younger sister and I had loving parents and, although they divorced when I was seven, it didn't have a particularly negative impact on me. I always felt very loved, and we certainly didn't want for anything growing up. I did well at school academically and was gifted with my father's genes at sport where I excelled. But still, I had chronically low self-esteem, was very lacking in confidence and this manifested itself in an eating disorder. In spite of this, I managed to get good enough grades to go to university, and it was during my time there, where I was suddenly away from the strict confines of home and watchful eye of my mother, that it really took hold of me. It certainly affected my experience of being at university, as I missed so many lectures and tutorials and, although I had a good friendship circle and a boyfriend, my eating disorder consumed me. I also partied hard, drank too much, like most other students, and just about scraped through the next four years, with a disastrous year interlude in France as a teaching assistant, which is a whole other story.

I graduated in 1992 with a passable 2:2 with no idea of what career I wanted to pursue or any real plan of what to do next, other than being determined to go to London, where I believed that things would somehow magically fall into place!

My friend and I arrived in London with big dreams,

but first we needed to find a job. It was pre-internet in those days, so we scoured the newspapers looking for jobs to apply for, trawled the length of various roads looking for bar and waitressing jobs, and in the meantime continued the obligatory drinking and partying. It was during a night out that we met a couple of guys who worked in publishing and they managed to secure us an interview at Haymarket Publishing, which is a big publishing company in Teddington. We went along to the assessment centre and sat through a whole day of interviewing and assessments, which I must admit I really enjoyed. At the end of it all, I was offered a job in telesales, selling advertising space on one of their premium titles, *Autocar & Motor*. My friend didn't get offered a job, which she wasn't unduly concerned with as she had loftier ideas and ended up on the other side of the fence working as an accounts executive for a big advertising company. My starting salary was the grand total of £9000 per year plus commission, which even back then was barely enough to survive on, but I didn't mind as I had a job, and it was the start of an exciting new chapter in my life.

Without knowing the first thing about cars, I found that I was good at talking to people and I thrived in a competitive environment. Although I didn't love telesales, I did love the whole team and social aspect that came with it, and that job was the start of a career in sales, which segued into recruitment a few years later.

Back in the nineties, working in recruitment in London was a bit like working on the trading floor of a bank and, in fact, it was not unlike the film with Leonardo Di Caprio, *The Wolf of Wall Street*, although maybe not quite as hedonistic! It was definitely work hard and play even harder and I found I was very good at doing both. I was earning close to six figures and again I thrived on the competition and I loved the people I was working with, but the hours were long and there was always the underlying pressure that if you didn't perform you were out. In addition, my eating disorder continued to wreak havoc on my life and that, coupled with burning the candle at both ends, took a definite toll on my physical and mental health, and I ended up taking huge amounts of time off work and, on my darkest days, I even considered ending things.

Looking back, I would love to scoop that Sarah up and give her a big hug and persuade her to do things differently. I was spending the money I was earning as fast as it was coming in, mainly on binge food, drink and drugs, and if I wasn't in the middle of a food binge or fasting episode, I was out drinking and partying. I put myself in some horrifically dangerous situations and I'm so grateful that nothing truly bad ever happened to me. It's a miracle too that I managed to hold down a job, and not only that, be really successful at it. At the core of it, I was deeply unhappy and unfulfilled, but I didn't know how to break free from the cycle I was in.

Things continued like this to varying degrees for several years and, in the meantime, I held down a couple of long-term relationships as well as some shorter-term ones, always with highly unsuitable men; I got engaged three times, moved to Birmingham for several years and went back to London, and then in 2011 my mother was diagnosed with myeloma, which is a type of blood cancer. This was a really pivotal time in my life, as suddenly the person who I adored, who loved me unconditionally and was the one person I could always truly count on, could be taken away from me.

After several weeks of travelling back and forth to Leicestershire at weekends to see her, I decided to quit my job and flat in London and move back, so that I could be with my family, which also meant leaving the well-paid recruitment job I was in. After much soul searching, I decided that I didn't want to work for any of the recruitment companies in the Midlands, as I had had enough of working for other people, and I decided to set up my own recruitment firm working from home. I have always found in my life that when something is meant to be, things tend to happen quite organically and naturally, and when it's not, it's like wading through treacle. My three engagements and planning for the weddings were like wading through treacle, hence they never happened, thank goodness, while setting up my own business was not; in fact, it was the complete antithesis. Within weeks, I had got everything in place and within the first two months I had made my first placement.

I absolutely loved working for myself, as it gave me the flexibility I needed to spend time with my mum, it got me out of the rat race and away from the destructive and unhealthy lifestyle that I had still been leading and was quite frankly sick of. I can't tell you how relieved I was to be away from London and the relentless pressure that I was under. I would absolutely dread Mondays and walking to the Tube station those mornings would make me feel physically sick. Being back home in Leicestershire, after living away for so long, felt like being enveloped in a giant, warm hug, in spite of my mum being so ill. I moved back into my childhood home with her and my stepfather and I'm so grateful for the time I got to spend with Mum, as sadly, in February 2012, she passed away. She was a truly amazing woman, as she never once complained, and she was unequivocally the wisest and kindest person I've ever known.

After she died, we were all a bit adrift, but at least I had the business to focus on. I moved into my own flat in the same village as my sister and her family, which was only a few miles away from my stepdad, and life went on. I reconnected with old friends and cherished the time I had back with my family, my recruitment business was doing all right and even though Mum had gone, I felt happier than I had in a long while. My eating disorder still reared its ugly head, but it was a lot more manageable than before and, although I still drank too much, I had stopped doing drugs and was living a much healthier lifestyle. Having been so good at sport at school, I got back into fitness and took up running again, and I think I would have carried on like this indefinitely until November 2012, when my now husband, who I had actually met in 2008, came back into my life and everything turned upside down again. A year later, I moved back to Birmingham so that we could live together, as his work and two children were there and the nature of my business gave me that flexibility, and my life turned the next corner.

Although I really missed my family and my life in Leicestershire, it was great being back in Birmingham, as it really is my favourite city in the UK. Everything you need is on your doorstep and I gradually built a strong network of work clients and candidates and my recruitment business flourished. The only downside was not having a team of people around me to bounce off and working from home could be very isolating. In addition, although I had made a very good living from recruitment, I had never loved it and I have always had this nagging feeling that I could be doing something much more fulfilling. But what could I do without completely retraining that would give me the flexibility and income that my current business did? It was a question that I had asked myself a thousand times over the years but had never found the answer to.

In 2018, my husband and I started talking about going into business together, batting different ideas back and forth about what we could do. He was burnt out from working in social care and I was stuck in my recruitment rut and definitely ready for a change. My husband is actually a professional artist with an amazing talent for art and creativity and he had always wanted to go back to it, so we decided to have a look at setting up our own art gallery business.

In much the same way as when I set up my recruitment business, fate took charge, the stars aligned and before we knew it, we had found and signed a lease on an amazing space in Birmingham city centre. The Birmingham Contemporary Art Gallery was born and had its launch night in December 2019.

Without knowing the first thing about art or owning an art gallery, I found my recruitment head kicked in, and I took charge of the things that I could do, such as setting up a business from scratch, networking, building a database of clients and basically selling! The rest I am learning along the way and I also have a very good teacher in my husband whose knowledge of the art world is second to none. In the last twelve months, even in spite of lockdown, the business has evolved into developing programmes that use art to support those with mental health issues and we have set up a not for profit arm to run alongside the gallery called The heARTivism Project, whose aim is to support cultural and artistic projects while tackling issues that reduce social and creative inclusion for minority communities. We have had fantastic feedback from so many different people and it's incredible to finally be doing something that feels worthwhile. It's been scary and very challenging at times, because it's so far out of my comfort zone, but I absolutely love it and I feel like it's saved my own mental health.

I also made the decision in 2019 to stop drinking, as I felt that it had become too much of a crutch and it was having a negative impact on my health and state of mind, plus I knew in my heart that I was addicted. I have always been an all or nothing person and done things to extremes, and I knew the best thing for me was to stop altogether. Once I made the decision, it was surprisingly easy.

In August 2020 I turned fifty and coming up to my fiftieth birthday was definitely a defining milestone. I knew that if I didn't stop bingeing and throwing up, I would still be doing it when I was in my seventies or eighties, if I even lived that long. In reality, I would have ended up having a heart attack or dying of throat cancer and I couldn't in all consciousness continue to do something that had such a detrimental effect on my health and well-being. After the initial therapy that I had when I was sixteen, I tried various other treatments and therapists over the years up until my late thirties, but nothing ever worked, and I had pretty much given up hope and accepted that it was something I would always live with and have to manage.

That is, until I read a book called *Brain Over Binge* by Kathryn Hansen, which was quite literally a light bulb moment for me because it was as if she were me. She described situations and thoughts that completely mirrored my own and it made me realise what I had always suspected, that my eating disorder was an incredibly bad habit that I had allowed to take over my life and it was an addiction, just like drugs or alcohol or any other addiction, and in order to overcome it, I needed to completely rewire my brain. It wasn't instantaneous and it took me until three months before my fiftieth birthday to say enough was enough. If I could give up drinking, I could do this, and since 25th May 2020 I have been

THE ELEVATION OF THE *Femalepreneur*

free from my eating disorder. The feeling of liberation that I have is indescribable. I feel weightless, like I have thrown off the shackles of this awful addiction and I am now finally living my life.

My grandmother always said, 'what's for you won't go by you' and I truly believe that this is the case. It's never too late to follow your dreams and live your life and it's all about timing. I just took a bit longer to get there than some others and that's okay.

***

Sarah Wallace lives in Birmingham with her husband Albert and rescue lurcher Marcy and is stepmother to two beautiful children. She is Director of her own recruitment company, Saffron Resourcing, and co-founder and owner with her husband of The Birmingham Contemporary Art Gallery. She is passionate about helping and bringing people together and, when she isn't working, you will find her out walking the dog or with her nose stuck in a book! These days her mantra is very much around living life to the full and, to quote Richard Branson, "If someone offers you an amazing opportunity but you are not sure you can do it, say yes – then learn how to do it later!"

You can find Sarah here:

https://www.instagram.com/thebcag/
https://www.instagram.com/sarahjanewallace1/
https://www.instagram.com/theheartivismproject/

# Hold On to Hope
## Kirsty Gravett

*I dedicate my chapter to Chris. My love, my soulmate and best friend. May you dance with the angels and guide us with your loving ways. I also dedicate this chapter to our incredibly strong children. You give me reason to breathe, you boys are my absolute world.*

We had it all. We thought we had forever. Chris and I were young, we had two young boys and I was pregnant with our third child. We were excited about what the future had in store for us but, ultimately, we were beginning to plan our wedding, which we had decided to put on hold because we wanted to buy a house. We wanted a house of our own. Our family home. We purchased our first home together back in late 2016. Excited was an absolute understatement! The last few years of saving, working long hours, and being so careful with money had paid off! We did it! We now had our own home. The boys loved it! Now with baby number three on the way, things were just getting better and better for us. Chris and I were soulmates, we loved each other incredibly. Our boys were a reflection of the immense love we had for each other, and the love we had for each other just grew and grew.

We lived for each other and our boys, our perfect little family. Nothing was going to stop us, we had the world at our feet. With all of us together, we were going to conquer it all. We were happy and healthy. This was OUR time.

Except it wasn't.

On the 3rd of October 2017, Chris had a heart attack during the early hours of the morning. It happened out of the blue, he had no pain, no warning. I felt something wasn't right when he woke me up not long after he had got home from a long shift at work. He had said over the weekend that he didn't feel quite right, but perhaps he was just coming down with a cold or something. My gut instinct was telling me to call an ambulance, and within the space of an hour, my house was filled with paramedics. The lights from the ambulances were flickering through the closed curtains as our boys slept in their beds. I remember standing on the landing, hoping and praying that everything was going to be okay. But I was worried, there was a sense of calm in the air, despite one of the paramedics running up and down the stairs frequently bringing in yet more equipment. Radios were going off, the air ambulance was circulating, more paramedics arrived. The noise from the defibrillator will be a noise that will haunt me for the rest of my life.

"Stand clear, preparing to shock... Shock administered."

In that moment I knew EXACTLY what was

happening. He was being resuscitated. The door to our bedroom could never shut properly. Chris used to make digs at the vast number of handbags and scarfs that were hanging on the back of the door but, through the crack in the door, I saw a mass of green uniforms working over him. Monitors and wires were continually being applied to him, medications were being administered with mutterings amongst the paramedics, but I couldn't work out what they were saying. One paramedic, a young lady, placed her hand on my shoulder and said, "We're doing all that we can." She knew that I knew. This situation very rarely has a positive outcome. Ever. The paramedics were angels, they did everything they could to stabilise Chris enough to enable him to be transferred to hospital.

You see intensive care units on the television and instinctively know that they are extremely critical places to be. Walking through the corridor of the intensive care unit to see Chris was such a very surreal experience. It was calm, there was no chaos. The machines bleeped here and there, the nurses were attentively looking after their patients whilst doctors examined charts and scans in hope of finding something that will enable them to give a little positive news to the relatives.

Chris lay in the hospital bed covered head to toe in tubes, wires and machines and, even though he was showing good signs of healing from the heart attack, his brain was not. The doctors did scan after scan after scan. There was no brain activity. The nurses knew that I was pregnant and were concerned about me and the baby too, they always made sure I had eaten that day. I held Chris's hand, and with all that I am and was, just hoped and prayed that he would give me a sign that he was going to be okay. He needed to be okay. We had our third child on the way, we had plans, we had our lives ahead of us. We needed him with us. Our family and friends needed him.

The next few days were an absolute blur. Taking the long drive to the hospital every day whilst trying to maintain some sort of normality for the boys, with friends and family helping in every way they could. I was on autopilot, not really making sense of what was really going on or what was being said. I just could not get my head around the fact that my soulmate, the father of my children, was on a life support machine. This can't be happening. Not now. Not ever. But it was happening, and in a split second, Chris took his last breath on the 6th of October 2017.

Our world came crashing down. The light in our lives had gone forever. For a while I felt like this was an incredibly bad dream and that I was going to wake up and see his cheeky face grinning back at me. But it wasn't a bad dream. This was reality. My reality. Our reality. I was crushed. Heartbroken.

Telling our boys that their dad had died was the hardest thing I have ever had to do. That broke me even more. Seeing their little hearts break into pieces, tears filling their eyes. Their worlds had come crashing down. Daddy had gone.

A split second can change everything.

The next few months were a blur. I just existed in a

bubble. The world wasn't the same anymore, but with every month that passed, the baby inside me was developing. I needed to be strong for our boys and for the child that Chris would never get the chance to meet. I knew I had to be strong, but my heart was broken. Our futures had been taken away. All those dreams and plans we had were no longer there. It had all been taken away in a split second. I am so thankful to our family and friends for all of their love and support that they gave endlessly in the weeks, months and years afterwards. I genuinely feel that things would have been so different if the boys and I didn't have such a strong support network. And for that I am so blessed.

It's such a hard thing to try and comprehend. When the person you have spent the last decade with is no longer there. The texts, the phone calls, the little quirky things that he did. The affection, the support, your happily ever after. It's all gone. Forever. How could we ever possibly live our lives without him?

A few months after Chris died, the company that I was with rolled out an incentive. The chance to earn a branded trunk. But I dismissed the opportunity because I just wasn't focusing on anything other than trying to get through each day. This incentive just wasn't at the forefront of my mind at the time. But things started happening. I began to see feathers, robins, rainbows, heart-shaped clouds in the sky. Even certain songs that Chris and I used to listen to began to play more frequently. What was going on? Was this a sign? The more I dismissed the idea of running for this incentive, the more signs and synchronicities I would receive.

Chris was always my biggest cheerleader when it came to my little business. He supported me right from the start. In fact, he was the one who suggested I joined. Back in 2015, Chris came home from work with a scratch card for us both. To my surprise, I won £100. We were so excited. At the time, we were desperately saving for a deposit for our house, so any extra money that came through was quickly put into our savings account. But, on this occasion, Chris said "No". He was such a kind-hearted and generous soul and insisted that I treated myself. He kept saying, "Buy that kit you've had your eye on. If you want it, have it. Now is your chance."

I took the plunge and signed up. He was so proud of my little business and supported me in every way. MLM can be a tough world and, during the times that I was ready to give up, he always encouraged me to keep going. He saw how much more this opportunity was, it wasn't just a little side hustle. It was bigger than that. This had begun to help the struggles that I had with my self-confidence and feelings of self-doubt. I was doing something that ignited a passion from within and this was something that I had never ever done before. He was my biggest cheerleader, and he even shared the same passion as me to hopefully, one day, earn that elusive branded trunk!

The signs that kept coming woke something up inside of me. This was something that I had never really experienced before. I couldn't explain it. Was this Chris cheering me on from a spirit realm? Despite feeling at rock bottom, I began to show up. I began to gain strength both physically and mentally. I suddenly felt a little more hopeful. I felt like the sun was beginning to break through the dark, lonely clouds. Maybe this was my chance? Maybe Chris was trying to tell me something?

It wasn't easy. It was never going to be easy, but somehow, I knew that this was what I needed to do. This is what Chris would've wanted me to do. Despite everything, I earnt it! I was absolutely over the moon but, at the same time, incredibly upset as Chris wasn't there to celebrate with me.

Grief is a terribly difficult and lonely journey. The lows can literally sweep you off your feet and you feel like you are back to square one again. The pain of losing someone hurting through every single cell of your body. With every breath you take. Grief will never go away. But it's how you begin to live this new life that reduces the intensity of how grief feels. When that grief wave happens, I now acknowledge it, rather than letting it engulf every single cell within my body. I used to let it consume me because it's easier to feel the pain of losing the absolute love of my life than even consider living a life without him in it.

My thought process changed when I began to look at my own mindset. Grief is a sign of the love that once was. The incredible love that Chris and I had for each other. This gave me hope. Hope can be delivered in so many ways and, by taking a little positivity from each day, will help you work through your feelings. I take my signs of hope from the messages that I receive from Chris in a spiritual format. I also look at the strength and resilience that our children have shown, how they have tried to understand what has happened to us but, at the same time, how they have continued to live their lives. Their successes at school, the wins they have had with their favourite activities, watching our baby develop... these are all little signs of hope. And I embrace every single one of them because, actually, life is so very precious and all it takes is a split second for that all to change.

Since Chris died, I have felt drawn to walk down a spiritual path. During my pregnancy I began to have reiki treatments, I also began to research the healing benefits of crystals. I was hopeful that this was going to help with the shock and trauma of Chris's death. I was incredibly worried about whether my heartbreak would affect our unborn child and I needed alternatives.

The spiritual journey continued, and I began to explore other things such as journaling, moon rituals, angelic healing and using crystals to try and ease the tremendous heartache that was present not only in my heart but also deep within my soul. The change within myself has been a powerful one and not only on a personal level but I feel it brings me closer to my cheerleader, Chris, on a spiritual level.

When you walk this path, you start to become aware of things and situations happening for a reason. Maybe the reason is unknown at the time, but these things have a habit of working out if you just believe. And believe in YOU. People enter our lives and can help in so many ways and this is exactly the case with two beautiful souls, Jo and Natasha. I am so thankful to them for crossing my path because they have been able to guide me further spiritually and also give me the tools required to open up my heart and soul, release those deep-rooted emotions associated with Chris's death, which, in turn, has helped me to begin to see a brighter future. A brighter future not just for me but for our beautiful boys too.

Three years ago, I never envisaged where I would be right now. I never could imagine feeling the sun on my cheeks, smiling with a deep sense of adoration for our three wonderful children and at the same time holding Chris firmly in my heart. He was and always will be our superhero.

For anyone reading this and is feeling like their whole world has crashed around them. To feel that there is no light around you. To feel like you have no purpose or any sense of being or belonging. Just be patient with you. You are needed. You are loved.

There is always hope.

★★★

You can find Kirsty here:

www.naturalbeautybykirsty.com
https://www.facebook.com/naturalbeautybykirsty/
https://www.instagram.com/naturalbeautybykirsty/

# I Want to be Free Said the Little Girl In Me

## Louise Misell-Joseph

*My chapter is firstly dedicated to my children to show them that anything is possible if you put your heart and soul into it. You're all amazing humans and I love you to the moon and back.*

*Also, I'm dedicating to my soulmate, my husband Leroy, who has been my rock through thick and thin. Your support is endless, I'm so lucky to have found you. Thanks for being you, I love you dearly.*

*Then to my number one gorgeous granddaughter, words cannot tell you how much I love you and I want you to know the world is your oyster, you can be anyone you want to be and while I have breath in my body I will support you 100%. BE FREE.*

I was pushed and shoved from pillar to post through my childhood. I was a little girl, an only child. I was so very lonely. I know I have lots of my memories that are hidden deep, because if I opened the memory it had something awful attached, so I shut it down. Have you ever felt like this, if you ignore it, it isn't real? This is what I thought, I will lock them in a box and then it won't affect me.

How wrong was I?!

So, I grew up not knowing my mother was an alcoholic and my dad was a womaniser. Although the little girl inside me thought something was wrong, there was no one to talk to.

I remember around the age of five, Dad wasn't around anymore. I didn't know why he wasn't around, but it was just me and Mum and we moved around a lot. I felt lost and unsettled. I do have a nice memory; I remember receiving the most beautiful handwritten Disney illustrations in letter form from Dad. They brought great joy to me. He mentioned he would be home soon. I didn't understand where he was, I felt scared. I didn't know how long he was away for; time was irrelevant. Was this normal? It didn't feel it. Dad mentioned about going to visit the cinema to watch the films that he had illustrated in his letters, I have memories of this happening.

Whilst Dad was away, we went to a hotel to visit him. It was a big open space with lots of tables and pretty gardens and it was so nice to see my dad. Unbeknown to me, this was an open prison. I found out later in my parents' argument; this was a big shock. When Dad returned home, we moved again, and things seemed to be nice for a while, I think.

Then during a later argument, I found out that I had four older sisters. I was shocked, I wasn't meant to find out, it was meant to be a secret, but I now knew, they couldn't take that back. I wanted to see them. NO, I heard my mum say, which really upset me, I didn't understand and was told to shut up.

Wait, you're telling me I had been on my own, suffering all this time, and I had big sisters? Who were they? Was I going to meet them? So many questions, no answers.

The little girl inside me felt alone again. I kept pushing my feelings down.

I felt like I had been abandoned, but this time from strangers, who didn't know me, and they were my older sisters from Dad's first marriage. It felt like they didn't want to know me or want me.

Things were complicated, I was told never to speak of them again. The secret continued. A little girl with so many untold stories (secrets); I felt lost again.

Until I was in my late teens, just before I left home. After my siblings were born, I mentioned it again. Why was I not allowed to see them? Was I different? Why didn't my sisters want to meet me? I was so intrigued to meet them. The little girl in me was crying out for the love of my sisters for so many years. So many questions and NO ANSWERS. It continued to be locked away, yet again.

I remember when my mum was pregnant with my brother that she had a nervous breakdown, and ended up in hospital. I wasn't allowed to visit; I was very scared and feared I wouldn't see Mum again. My dad had to work, and he left me with all these young ladies who I didn't know. I just remember he said it was one of the office staff from his work. I never questioned anything but felt abandoned by my dad. Not knowing how Mum was, and not allowed to see her; I was only nine. What was happening? My world was turned upside down again. Is this how life was always going to be?

I'm not sure how long Mum was in hospital, but any length of time is too long without your mum at nine years old. Mum then went on to have my brother and later followed my little sister.

Did this mean we were a happy family now?

We had to move to a new house as well to make room for my siblings. Hopefully things would be stable now. Although all it did was bring more poverty to our house, too many mouths to feed, and arguments started again.

Secondary school felt so hard. I didn't like one subject. I felt left out, ugly and overweight because I was developing into a woman well before the other girls. So people ridiculed me for this, which affected my confidence, which wasn't great already. I never got to go on school trips or even play an instrument. I felt so different, I knew I wanted more, but never felt good enough.

But inside me the little girl said YOU ARE... I was trying to escape but I couldn't find a way. I just didn't know where to look or what to do and wasn't guided.

Home life was full on, I became the second mum looking after my brother and sister, cleaning and ironing; now even to this day I hate ironing. I just felt like the hired help at times, a babysitter and cleaner.

So, I decided I was going to join the Women's Royal Navy. I left home at the age of eighteen to begin *my* life and let that little girl in me escape and live her dreams of happiness. This didn't last long. I hadn't dealt with issues of not feeling good enough, so I failed several times. Then, eventually my fight broke through, and I passed my training and started my career. I was starting to love the life I was in when I met a man; we later fell in love and started a family.

My parents then split up and things really didn't get any better. Alcohol, lies, etc., etc., etc.

During my marriage, I was feeling not good enough. I let a lot of people control my life at this point. I really didn't have a close relationship with my alcoholic mother and one of my elder sisters had decided she wanted to become a daughter and moved in with my dad, but didn't want to know us other children. I knew my siblings felt the same, very sad. So, I began my journey with my own family and went on to have three beautiful babies, but unfortunately, I also had two miscarriages, one of them very traumatic. Adding to my worthlessness, this and lots of other things had a big effect on my marriage and it broke down. Failed again. 'But the little girl said you need to fight for your children, girl.' I was the protector.

I was now riding the storm alone. Three beautiful children to nurture and not damage like I was. This was the most difficult job in my life.

I worked my ass off to bring bread to the table. Have you felt like this? I had five jobs around the children for a long time, but this wasn't working.

I tried and did what I could to support and bring my children up the best way I knew. None of us are perfect.

Fast forward a few years.

I was working at a local airport, where I loved the job I did. During the time at this job I was bullied, cheated on and put through a capability process to fight for my job, which took a year, and I became ill with stress-related asthma. All this I let happen to me because I felt I wasn't worthy of happiness or success, I felt life was just on a downwards spiral. With what fight I had, I fought to the end and with my job I settled the capability out of court. I won something. I can do this. Come on, girl, you've got this, I told myself.

Okay, now for a fresh start. This is my time now, I have brought my children up to be amazing adults and I now need to find me, so the adventure started again. I applied for lots of jobs, I wanted a job now for me. My choice, not just because I needed to put food in my children's mouths. My children were ready for leaving home. I went for an interview in the big world of London for the Olympics 2012. I went for a supervisor job, returned home and the following day I received a call to say I had made the 2012 but not for the job I went for, it was for a duty manager! WHAT?! I was jumping around the lounge, I couldn't believe someone thought I was good enough, finally. Things felt like they were changing, and I felt amazing.

Fast forward, during the Olympics I met my future husband, although he lived in London. I returned home after a few months away working and we developed our relationship long distance. For the first time in my life, I really felt loved and wanted, and he believed in me and I felt fantastic, but I did have the shit I locked away still. How could I trust all this wasn't going to change then just turn bad like the rest of my life? OMG it's there again, doubting myself. Louise, get over it, for goodness' sake.

So, between us for the next four years, we had four very close relatives' deaths, decided to get married and I decided to start my own business online. Something completely alien to me. I could feel passion I never had before building in me; was that the little girl now starting to see her life? Over the next two years I built a nice little turnover of business, but I felt held back still. One day, I saw a friend, she looked different, not weight-wise but different in her face. I asked, what have you done? She told me her secret. She had dealt with past demons. OMG, WHAT?!

How can I do this? I said to myself, I have a little girl inside me waiting to live her life, to blossom and fulfil her dreams. Is this what she is hiding from?

She explained how and I then took the plunge. I did work on me to get rid of all the baggage I had. Now this isn't a fast thing and it really tears you apart; all I know is it's been worth every minute. The therapy delved into my whole life. It helped me remove all the unwanted emotions that I had stored in me right back to that little girl who couldn't live her life; she just existed around the mess that had been dealt her. Now for the first time she was going to be free.

My goodness, I felt alive although empty, which is hard to explain to others. I then thought about my past in such a different way. I now can see my parents in a different light, my mum especially, she was just a lost child herself. She'd never found herself and now had passed away, which is so sad.

I'm determined by the work I've done and continue to do on myself, so that on my death bed I can say I did my best, I was good enough and my little girl was able to get out and explore her life. I continue every day to work on me, because I love the person I have become, the life I have, and I know I can really achieve goals and get to places I never thought I would be able to. I have a successful business with a lovely team that I feel I help every day from my experiences in life. My products, which I sample to others, have helped me, they motivate and I'm more confident with everything in life. My marriage is amazing and we both fully connect. My children are healthy and happy, and I even have a granddaughter who I adore and lots of grandfurbies. So, in the end yes, I had a pretty rubbish younger life that I couldn't shake off as I was a young woman. As time has passed by, I have started to love me and blossom and show my real worth. This is possible for us all, you just must believe and work on you.

So, when I decided to tell my story of the little girl inside me, I knew there were so many other ladies lost, broken, needing to read my story. I wish I had had this guidance. If you think you can resonate with my story, then I want to let you know you've got this, girl. Perhaps

I've made a difference by you reading this chapter, perhaps not, but what I do know is, you are capable of anything and YOU ARE ENOUGH. It took me a long time to find my way, but I'm now on the right track and loving sharing my story and helping others. From just having to care for me it helped me know what I want in life as well.

★★★

I want to make a difference to someone else's life. Is that you?

If you want to talk or sample your new you, you can find Louise here:

https://www.facebook.com/louise.misell
https://linktr.ee/louisemj
https://www.facebook.com/groups/louisemj/

# LIFE BEGINS AT FORTY, NEVER GIVE UP

## Marie Clout

*I dedicate my chapter to the women out there who have ever felt like they didn't belong, they didn't fit in, or who believed that nothing great was going to happen in their life.*

*To the people that inflicted this pain and trauma on me from a very young age, I thank you. It has taken me forty years to release this emotion that has been stored away, but you are the reason I get up every day, I show up and have become the woman that I am today.*

*To my soulmate, my husband, thank you for being my rock, always by my side, you are always so proud of me, my best friend, I love you, we have got this baby.*

*To my amazing family for helping me grow into the woman I am today, for showing me the way and for being there for me always, I thank you for your unconditional love.*

*To my little Nan, who is with the angels, it breaks my heart even writing this. Thank you for being a fundamental figure in my life from the day I was born, I love you always and forever.*

My heart was racing, beating out of my chest, I was shaking, I felt sick, I felt like I was going to pass out. In this moment of my life, I was running away from those horrible bullies at school. From a young age, I suffered from bullying, not always the physical bullying, but the words, the taunting, the words that I have relived through my whole life. It never goes away; you think it has, but it always rears its ugly head and starts to define you as a person until that is all you believe, those voices of those people, the anxiety and panic attacks, a lack of self-worth. Forty years on and I am finally at peace but it has not been an easy journey. I am now ready to share my story.

I loved school. I was quite an academic person, but I had to work hard at it. I loved nursery and primary school, growing up with some amazing friends. Our school classes were so close and we had great friendships, but then life moves on and secondary school started. I wasn't a confident girl, I was 6ft tall, suffered really bad acne and just generally wasn't the "cool girl" of the class, the one everyone wanted to be around. I wasn't the slimmest of girls either, so sports was not really my thing, especially running, so I just threw myself into my studies. I used to come home, be in my room, listening to my favourite songs to take me away from that lonely place, which was my own release. I spent a lot of time talking to my nan about the days at school and she was always there for a big hug; she never judged but gave good advice. Family life was good, we had nice things and we had lots of laughs, but then that would all disappear when it was time for school again. The time at the weekends always passed by so quickly.

My close friends made new friendships and that's when things started to change. They wouldn't spend lunchtimes with me, sit next to me in class, I just felt so alone. I didn't have a massive circle of friends, it wasn't something I found easy, meeting new people and socialising, it was all a bit awkward. The name calling would start and then I would be followed home from school, being taunted the whole way, to the point I would make myself sick running all the way home. The school bus filled me with dread. I couldn't sit upstairs as I wasn't "cool", I was just laughed at, it was a living nightmare. I felt my attendance at school was suffering, as I was waking up with tummy aches and anxiety at the thought of going to school. I finished school and completed my GCSEs, but I had to work hard for them for some reason. Exams didn't come naturally, I had to study hard for them. Again, nothing seemed to be easy for me and I felt like everyone was laughing at me all the time, 'Is she stupid or something?'

Let's fast forward a few years. I went to college for the first year and again the anxiety crept in. I just wanted to turn that voice off in my head but it was there all the time, constantly questioning myself that I wasn't clever enough to be there, even though my lifelong dream of being a teacher could keep me on track. After my first year, I left college. I felt a huge sense of disappointment and that I had let my family down; I was supposed to

88          THE ELEVATION OF THE *Femalepreneur*

be the first daughter to go off to university. For some reason, something was saying 'it's not for you'. Again, I felt my lack of confidence holding me back. I wasn't making friends, I wasn't fitting in, what was wrong with me?! I couldn't even tell my parents I had left college. I made excuses that I had a free lesson or wasn't going in until later. I had told my nan, she didn't judge, she just said, 'You need to do what makes you happy and I am proud of you whatever you decide.' I told my parents. Yes, they were disappointed, and said I would need to get a job and not sit around doing nothing. So I did, I went and got my first job, and my journey into retail had begun. Totally different to the path of teaching I was going to take, I didn't really know what I was doing, I was just a bit stuck in life and feeling lost, so had to start somewhere. I enjoyed what I was doing, I started to feel independent earning my own money, but then I hit a wild phase and would be out drinking every Friday and Saturday night with my work friends, and on the Saturday I wouldn't even go to work, my parents rang in sick for me.

What was I doing with my life? This wasn't the path I wanted to be on. The drinking was great at the time, a sense of confidence, I could do anything, was able to talk to people, have fun, laugh and joke, something I had never had before, but this wasn't good. It took me being rushed to hospital after drinking a lot and my drink being spiked for me to have a huge wake up call; I have never seen my parents so worried. I needed to stop and now. So, I did. I focused on my work and making new friendships, some of which I have to this very day. I got a few promotions at work, which was great, and I felt a real sense of achievement, but deep down I was still questioning myself. I wasn't good enough, what were people's perceptions of me? I was tested at work, it felt like they would pile on the pressure to see whether I was tough enough or if I would break, it was driving me crazy. It was really making me lack confidence in myself again, that I can't do this, that I'm not allowed to be successful and do well, that there will always be something to trip me up and laugh. I was not thirteen or fourteen years old anymore, I was nearly twenty. I needed to change but all I wanted to do was run and keep running. That was my defence; if I ran then I would be safe and I didn't need to think or worry and didn't have to face up to anyone or anything.

Things needed to change again and oh they did. Out of the blue, I met my now husband. Our paths crossed at work and, within three months, he had proposed! Insane, you may say, but this was the biggest moment of clarity that I had had my whole life, that I wanted to be with this man for the rest of my life. Again, there were people's opinions, I was too young, take your time, but I remember my nan saying to me, "You can't help who you fall in love with," and that's so true. This was the starting point for me, I thought, to getting my life back on track and having a purpose. I was going to be a wife, I had responsibilities. This event in my life led me to handing my notice in and applying for a better job role in retail as we were buying our first house. I wrote out my new

THE ELEVATION OF THE *Femalepreneur*

CV and, although again in my head I thought 'don't be silly, you can't do that job', I applied, had the interview and, guess what? I got the job! I couldn't believe it. I was excited, I had got that job myself, I was buzzing. I knew that it would be a job I enjoyed, and I loved it.

Fast forward a few years on, I was twenty-six, we were happy, we had bought our house and set a date to get married, really happy times. Then things started up again at work. My kindness was abused, I was naive and felt like I was being used to further someone else's career. Things happened, I was bullied mentally and it was not good for me, so I had to leave. I had hit rock bottom again and it made me really ill. My anxiety was at an all-time high and I couldn't understand why someone would do that to me, who I thought was a friend, and who had been a friend for nearly five years. I was sick for eight weeks, I wasn't eating, I was depressed. My family were worried, but I had a wedding to plan for, so was trying to gain the strength to get through that. I pulled the strength from somewhere and had the best wedding and married my soulmate in front of our family and friends. The best day of my life.

Once the excitement of the wedding and the honeymoon was over, I knew I had to focus on getting another job. Again, it's the process of getting yourself out there, feeling vulnerable, confidence low and wondering if people are going to want you for their business. Are you good enough? Marie, you cannot run from this, you need to face this head on. So, I applied for another job and amazingly they phoned me back the same day to offer me the job. It was great! I had a new job but for the past fifteen years I had been working so hard, pushing to be better, always working, having no time freedom. Feeling like I was just living to work and pay the bills. Feeling an outpouring of guilt that I was always at work, never really seeing my family and friends, just needing to be successful. My husband and I were like passing ships, we both worked in retail and had to catch a few moments together in the evenings or when we were getting ready for work. Our time off was our booked holidays when we could spend quality time together. Christmases were never really Christmas because one of us or both were always working.

Life moved on, years had gone by since then, I was getting older, in fact reaching my fortieth year. I still had a great job in retail, I just kept working and working, but it wasn't giving me everything I needed, I was just existing day to day. What was my purpose? Eat, sleep, work, repeat. I have had many promotions and a couple of side promotions where it felt like I was going backwards again and thinking why? What am I doing wrong? Here I go again, those voices in my head, the anxiety back. I was stuck, two steps forward, ten steps back, putting myself down all the time. Was it time that I needed to leave, however grateful I was for my career? Was it this telling me I needed another change? I didn't know how to do anything else, maybe it was those old doubts kicking in, getting on that school bus, everyone staring and talking about me, having an opinion and not knowing what that does to the person mentally.

I woke up one morning in January 2020 and knew that my life was going to go in another direction. I am a bit of a perfume lover, like a lot of us out there, and my hubby, bless him, bought me a couple of these bottles for Christmas. They were my favourite perfumes just packaged slightly differently. I wanted to get some more, so he put me in contact with a lady who was promoting them. We had swapped messages online and then she asked whether I would like to sign up to be a brand ambassador. I said to my husband it's not really for me, I am not a confident person, I am not a salesperson, I can't do that, but I wanted the perfumes, so I did a crazy thing and signed up. What did I just do? I haven't got enough time as it is and how can I balance everything? But I was only signing up for the perfume, so it was okay. I started talking to some of the other brand ambassadors for the company and had seen some of the success stories and I thought 'wow, this could change my life'. They said you needed to recruit but I didn't want to, so for the first eight weeks I didn't. However, just by me talking to friends and family I had sold a lot of perfume and in my first month I earned £300 commission plus a £400 bonus and my instant profit. I realised pretty quickly that my life could change, but still doing something I loved. I was still working full-time and starting to really build my business when I got my first couple of team members who wanted to achieve the same thing, have more time at home and a better work-life balance, which I had been craving. It was really nice to have a bit of extra income coming in for some nice treats. My family were so proud of me, my nan said she was proud and that I had done really well for myself.

My confidence was growing, and I felt an overwhelming sense of achievement. I was so far out of my comfort zone that there was no turning back. Then my world turned upside down. My family suffered incredible loss, my father-in-law passed away and then two weeks later my nan was taken away from us. I felt like my world had been destroyed. The one lady who had been present in my life had gone, I couldn't give her that final cuddle and tell her how much she meant to me, and then the guilt hit me again like a tonne of bricks. What if I hadn't been working all those hours? What if I'd had the time to spend with her? What if we could have seen my father-in-law more? Life is taken so quickly and it put my whole life into perspective; it's only taken a huge loss and my fortieth birthday this year to give me the kick that I needed.

Being off work for those months allowed me to really build my business online, and I did. The next few months were insane! I had my WHY firmly in everything that I did and I grew my team, coached them and I hit the top of my company's compensation plan for the first time. The feeling of pride and sense of achievement was incredible; I did that, I helped my team achieve that, I was shaking again, but not out of fear, out of the best emotion possible. I finally had found something for me, something that I am good at. Everything was going really well, my team and I continued to hit the top and my next goal was in sight. Then the next two months really slowed down and along came the disappointment again. I doubted myself once more, how had it gone wrong? Maybe it wasn't for me and I was just a dreamer, maybe I should just run away and not deal with it, give up and let those voices in my head win. But there was something in me. I wasn't prepared to give up with what I had started knowing what I could achieve for myself and my family.

I was stuck again in work, questioning everything I was doing, burying my head in the sand. I wanted to just disappear and then I was ill again. I lost a stone in a couple of weeks and was back in hospital; this time I knew for my health and my mindset I had to do something.

Having access to the internet and my online network, I was introduced to the Femalepreneur Academy by a friend in the same network marketing business. I thought maybe they could help me back to the path I was on. She sent me the link and I was looking at their online group page. It really resonated with me, the pain points I had been suffering from for years. Maybe they could help me with the ongoing voices, the past trauma of bullying that has affected my whole life, my lack of confidence and sudden anxiety in situations when they go wrong? So I took the biggest step to change my life around and I signed up to their monthly subscription and that is where I met JoJo and Natasha.

Following on from one-to-one calls and some timeline therapy, I felt an instant sense of calm. A weight had been lifted, I found me again, years of voices and opinions in my head, clouding my judgement and not being able to succeed and have the life I long for. I now feel like I can accomplish anything as, for the first time in my life, I believe in myself fully, I can see my future mapped out in front of me with crystal clear vision. I am only at the start of my journey, but I am so excited to see where I get to. They have set me on a path to self-discovery. I have started journaling, looking at my fitness and doing things for me, which make me happy, that give me a sense of purpose. I feel free for the first time to do what I want to do, to ignore the opinions and judgements that have plagued my whole life, free to be ME. I'm not perfect but I am ME and I have learnt to love myself for who I am.

Since being part of the academy, I have seen so many shifts in my mindset and all aspects of my life, confidence, purpose. I stand up for myself and am not ashamed to do it. I have a voice and I should be heard, instead of allowing those voices of my childhood to fully consume my life. These events in our lives, however painful, shape us, and it takes us a while to release all this pain, but it makes us who we are as individuals. It has made me who I am, I am stronger, confident and I'm a determined woman who can achieve anything.

If I could talk to my younger self for five minutes, I would say everything is going to be okay, Marie, you are going to be more than all right, believe in yourself, don't let anyone else bring you down. You are a shining light ready to help inspire others and you can wake up every morning knowing that what you are doing brings you joy, that you are happy and can exist fully knowing that all the fear you are feeling now will be worth the journey to happiness you have now.

If you can take anything from reading my story, don't give up, you are the key to unlocking the life you want and desire, you are important and enough, keep those dreams alive, make them a reality. I have been through a lot that has mentally changed my path in life and have had to go through that to be the woman I am today. Life is hard, things are never easy, but all you need to do is trust, believe and you will achieve great things.

★★★

You can find Marie here:

https://www.instagram.com/adoreaspireinspire
www.facebook.com/marieclout

# WHAT'S MEANT WILL NEVER PASS YOU BY

## Buckso Dhillon

*I dedicate this chapter to the one constant silent support in my life… my better half Nic.*

"Oh, I best get some money out for tomorrow," I said to myself as I passed the ATM machine in Swiss Cottage underground station. I made my way to the shop, got my cornflakes for the morning and walked the short distance to the block of flats I was living in for the next twelve months. (How expensive is it to rent a room in London??!)

As I turned the corner into the forecourt, I saw a slim figure hanging around the entrance to the flats. It immediately puts me on edge, although I don't feel threatened. I used my security fob to let myself in, as he slid out of the way, and made my way to the lifts. Looking back, as I was waiting for the lift to arrive, I noticed he'd got his leg wedged in the door so it didn't close. I was getting a little nervous, my heart started to race. I was pressing the lift button a little more fervently, wishing it'd hurry the f*ck up! Phew, it's here. The door

THE ELEVATION OF THE *Femalepreneur*

slid open, I jumped in and frantically pressed the close button, but of course this building was like something out of the seventies and it took an AGE for the door to slide across and, just as it seemed to meet the other side to close, a skinny arm jutted through the gap, stopping it from closing. The door slid back open and the other arm came up, holding a gun. SHIT!

It was the loitering lad from the doorway.

"Give me your bag," he ordered. Well! I just went into some sort of automated, mumsy mode, as I could tell/feel he was not very old, seveneteen or eighteen, maybe?

"NO, you can't take my bag," I stated with earnest, frantically thinking of ALL the inconvenience that would ensue, if I handed my 'life' over to him. (I mean our bags ARE our life, aren't they, ladies!?)

Then he said, "Give me your phone."

To which I replied the same, "No, no you can't have that." Again, thinking about the shit pit I'd end up in, not having a phone, and all the hassle it'd bring me, living here in London, on my own. I then put my hand up, in a way that spoke, 'hang on, hang on', as I remembered. I'd just drawn out £20 and it was obvious he was after money.

*Thank god!* I screamed inwardly. "Here, take this," as I fumbled around in my bag, whilst STILL holding onto my 1kg box of Cornflakes, with a GUN pointing me in the face. (I mean, why didn't I just drop 'em to the floor?!) Hilarious now, as I'm recounting events! But not at the time. You see, this was meant to be the

BEST year of my life. Forty-two years old, making my WEST END debut, living in London away from life as I knew it. As an actor, this was meant to be the 'piece de resistance', right? Yet here I was, three months into my year-long contract, night before the BIG night known as 'PRESS night', where all the papers come along with a select bunch of celebrities, and 'little old me', who'd never had a day at drama school, never mind NO quals leaving school, was going to play MY part in the brand new, amazing musical based on the blockbuster movie, *Bend It Like Beckham*. So, why was it ME being mugged at gunpoint right NOW?! I'd only been living there three months, missing my eleven-year-old twins and husband I'd left behind in Derbyshire; wasn't that sacrifice enough? Wasn't I 'paying my dues' already with the loneliness and uncertainty of West End theatre life with NO ONE to count on, or trust? Didn't that negate me from any curveballs?

Obviously not. He took the money, just as the alarm on the lift went off, and the door started to close (in THAT moment, I genuinely thought my angels had raised the alarm or something like that but no, it was defo just because the lift door was being wedged open for too long), as he pulled back with his parting statement, "Call the police, and I'll kill you!" (Yeah? But how would you have found me?) I raced up to the seventh floor flat I was renting and broke down to my flatmate, who was just mortified and horrified that this had actually happened to me. As he said, in the fifteen years he'd been coming and going, and ten years living there, there was never any news of this sort of thing happening to anyone. Great. Just my life lesson then, eh? Thanks, Universe! You're really making me pay for wanting this dream, aren't ya? Yeah.

Anyway, a few weeks went by, and I was getting ready to head back to London from Derby, as I usually did on a Monday afternoon, when I started to feel really scared and, out of the blue, this nauseating feeling came over me and tears just started pouring down my face, as my heart raced. This in itself really frightened me because I'd never had anything like it happen before. And then in that moment I realised, this must be what they call having a panic attack. Even though I'd cried over the mugging, I never felt really threatened, so I didn't think I was still affected by it. Wow. My body obviously had other ideas. I got through it, though, pulled myself together and made my way down as usual, on the train. And as I was sitting there, looking out of the window, I thought back to my youth when, at thirteen years old, I realised that I actually had a singing voice.

This came about when I was asked to sing the theme tune to a popular eighties kids' show called *Why Don't You?* I could not believe it! The feeling I got from being in that studio. WOW! The front cover of our local paper and then on page seventy-seven of the *Radio Times*. Wowee, I loved this. Yes! This was going to be the life for me. But I was brought down to earth very, very quickly with a humungous bump.

I remembered, I'm one of six kids, middle child

growing up in a first-generation Indian immigrant family, meaning HUGE blocks and obstacles. My dad, bless him, had his hands full trying to feed and clothe a family of eight, never mind my high-falutin' fantasies of being an actor! But I just knew this was what I was GOOD at. I mean, I'd taken Music, Art and Drama at school, surely that was an indication of my creative streak? So, in short, I had no support, no cheerleaders backing my dreams. And this continued to be the case pretty much all of my life. Until, one day, a close family friend introduced me to a chap that was setting up his own agency in London.

Now, at this point, I'd only ever done extra work in the background, pottering about just loving being on set, never once thinking I would ever make it in front of the camera as a mainstream actor. So, I was very, very surprised when he suggested, back in 2008, that I should go and audition for this guy, which I did, after making sure that he'd fully explained to him everything about my qualifications, not going to drama school, et cetera, et cetera. To which he said, "Yes, very much so, but I still think this guy will love what you're able to do." So, I went and auditioned for him in September 2008 very, very badly, but I took direction well, and he definitely must have seen something in me because he took me on there and then and, three months later, I landed my first acting role in *Coronation Street*, as the registrar that married Tony and Karla!

Now the rest, as they say, is history and I've since gone on to appear in ALL of the UK soaps, except *Holby*

*City*, and *Corrie* has been four times now, holding a very special place in my heart.

I also appeared in the blockbuster Disney film *Aladdin*, back in 2019. Along with shows like *Unforgotten* series 2, *Last Tango in Halifax* and *Silent Witness*, to name a few. You see, because I left school with no qualifications, my dad's uneducated opinion suggested I'd be best helping him in his business, seeing as though I wasn't really academic enough to go to college. This is what life pretty much ended up being about for me, running Dad's off licence up until I was twenty-four years old, when I got my very first paying job. Oh, how I longed to be earning my OWN money!

I'd waited thirty-eight years to become an actor. My lifelong ambition. Now, if I'd known at sixteen years old that it would take me this long, I'd never have pursued it. You know, sometimes we don't always need to know when the universe is going to deliver to us. Because if we did have all the dates for our dreams coming true, where would we get the desire to fuel our dreams from?!

Having left school with no qualifications and no idea how I'd ever make it as an actor with just a burning desire to be on stage, I was just shunted from pillar to post with no obvious path to take from my current life. But still, the universe had its plans for me. And they came to pass because I stayed on track, in my lane, just holding that vision in my mind, in my heart.

It took three years and two failed auditions to get the part, then finally, on my third attempt for the West End show, I got a yes from the producers. But I realised by then, I didn't want it. By then, I'd had enough after three years of trying and I didn't really want to live without my family, in London, for a year, at the age of forty-two. I mean, it's something you do when you're younger, in your twenties, isn't it? Along with all the other hopefuls and dreamers, not with the weight of life hanging round your neck. But, of course, I had to because this was what it was all about, wasn't it?! This was what almost every actor wants, and for me to allow my fear to take over and stop me from going forward would have made ALL of what I'd gone through be for nothing.

All I know is that what's meant for you will never ever pass you by. But only if you stay on track. All of this had to come at a price, now I'm reflecting on it. Along the way, I've had to make some huge sacrifices because the people and situations in my life were never going to help me get where I wanted. I'm someone who HAS to seek her own truth, find out for herself whether something is going to work, or not.

That meant I had to leave behind my family, culture, identity and life as I knew it because of the choices I made in life, being of Indian descent. My choice in marrying my Caucasian husband didn't go down very well, which I totally accepted and understood, but was profoundly saddened by. So, I moved away, but it seemed life was to continue throwing many setbacks and obstacles my way. Thereafter, within four years of meeting my husband to be:

I'd lost my family.

His brother died.

We got married.

We had twins.

Woah, slow down, girl! Yeah, I know. I really know how to do the whole all or nothing thing, right? So, as you can imagine, many attempts were made by the universe, in life, to put me off course in my pursuit of my acting ambition, but I still harboured the dream and realised it wasn't going away. When the twins were around six or seven years old, I felt this huge void within me and I realised I was unfulfilled. This wasn't what I signed up for, an uneventful life of mediocrity and boredom. Now, don't get me wrong, I loved my babies and life with my gorgeous hubby with ALL my heart, but that's not all I was. There were facets, many facets of me not being revealed and I needed to fix that. The burning desire was still there to tread the boards and I just KNEW if I didn't at least exhaust that avenue I'd regret it for the rest of my days.

After all these years of feeling lost, like I was flotsam and jetsam being shunted from job to job, starting out after having the twins as a receptionist, then onto Asda checkouts, a call centre, then beauty therapist, to waking at 3.30am to work as an agency fragrance consultant at the airport, I just HAD to look into the world of acting and see just where it was I could actually fit in. I'd already decided it was better than nothing when I thought I'd give background work a go. I felt that by just being ON set as a supporting artiste was more than I could ever hope for, especially now I was nearing forty with still NO qualifications to speak of or any whiff of a drama school in sight. So, I did just that. For eighteen months. Before that fateful day meeting my future (and current) agent, whom I still have all these years later, 'cos I owe him. He took a chance on me and it paid off. God!! Never in a million years did I think I'd be able to get into acting with NO qualifications, never mind the fact I was living in Derbyshire. I mean, you're supposed to be living in the Big Smoke in London in order to be an actor, aren't ya?! SO, I'm gonna say it again, "What's meant for you, will never pass you by."

★★★

*From Cornershop to West End: One Woman's Tale of Success Through Adversity.*

That, ladies and gents, is the title of my upcoming book, in which I fill in ALL the gaps of my life's ongoing journey, in seeking fulfilment and living a life IN purpose. We only have ONE crack of the whip. If you REALLY want THAT thing you're chasing, you HAVE to go for it in spite of what's going AGAINST you! I have ZERO regrets and YES, I'd say I've achieved what I set out to do. How prepared ARE you, to go get IT?

DO you really want that thing you're coveting? Then make the choices and sacrifice whatever you have to, knowing it's ALL for YOU!

You can find Buckso here:

www.instagram.com/thevibrantsage
https://www.facebook.com/unearthyourdiamond

# YOUR DESTINATION AWAITS
## *Jenna Leigh*

*Mum, thank you for being the best role model that I could have wished for, for making me believe that everything is possible and that dreams really can come true! I will always be reaching for the stars and following that rainbow!*

To the girl who knows her destination awaits but the bumpy road is making you question your instinct, keep going! I did!

As a little girl I saw my mum working twelve-hour days, six days a week with commitment and dedication to give us a better life! THIS was my first limiting belief! Working hard and long hours meant a roof over your head and food on the table. There wasn't much past the beans on toast and a rented terraced house, but that's where limiting belief two came from, to appreciate what we did have and to not dwell on what we didn't have!

My mum was a single parent to me from the age of six, and I watched her work so hard with blood, sweat and tears just to keep up with the monthly rent payments. My mum, my best friend, gave me the best life possible and showered me not with gifts, treats, money and a wealthy childhood, but with love, respect, appreciation and a belief to follow my dreams.

From a young age I was introduced to confident communication. My mum owned a hairdressing salon and with my mum leaving clients mid colour to collect me from school, she would bring me back to the salon where, at the age of six, I learned how to talk to others confidently and how to hold a conversation. This is where my curiosity for conversations and people began! I would help my mum tidy the hair on the floor, and as I got older, I would make the tea. I knew the regulars, even started washing their hair, and this was my first introduction to the working life! And I loved it!! I would sit there for hours in the salon, talking, listening and watching. I was mesmerised and before I knew it, I was becoming a young little lady with lots of passion and ambition for working in a job that was rewarding and didn't feel like work.

I didn't do very well academically at school; I was a day dreamer! Dreaming of my first job, dreaming of earning my own money so my mum didn't have to work so many hours, dreaming of meeting new people and working for myself!

At the age of eleven, I came home and said, 'Mum, I've got a job.' This wasn't such a surprise to my mum with her knowing my ability to talk to people; she had no doubt that if I wanted something, I would work hard to get it. I went to the local farm down the road from where we lived and asked them if they wanted any volunteers. I had my first experience of approaching someone new, in a professional adult manner, and bagged myself some volunteer work helping with the visitors on the farm. This was an achievement for me! After a few weeks, I soon got disinterested and went back to helping my mum out at her salon and enjoying my school social life.

I made it through my GCSEs, not with the best grades, but with the best memories, experiences and life lessons. Again, when I reached secondary school, I didn't really have an interest academically, but I had an interest in making lots of friends, being sociable and getting by with my school work. 'The best days of your life', as every adult human told me at the time, and now I totally agree!

It came to the end of the last year at school and I had lots of wants, dreams and aspirations! At the age of sixteen, I didn't really know which path I wanted to take. I wanted to be a nursery nurse, a teacher, a manager, have my own beauty salon and be a nurse! I chose to go to college and do Beauty – I believe this came from my background with my mum, growing up with the salon life and I envisioned my life being the same. Why not, it did make me happy being in a room with like-minded ladies that loved to chat whilst being made to feel beautiful and confident!

I committed to a two-year course and I was so excited to get started! I started off really well with distinctions on every assignment and practical assessment (which was a shock to me with not getting great grades at school). I made lots of lovely new friends and I loved the freedom and independence. After one year, I said to my mum, 'I don't want to go to college anymore, Mum, I want to get a job.' My mum again, at this point, already knew my forever changing ambition and sat with me working through the pros and cons of staying at college or getting a job. We came to the conclusion that my strong-minded head was ready to stand on its own two feet and that I was old enough and wise enough to make my own decisions, and so I quit. This is where my journey began into the big wide world of work and forever quitting!

My first job was in a health store, stacking shelves, counting stock, working on the tills and I had a very abrupt, rude and disrespectful manager! The excitement of getting a job had soon vanished and I questioned if I should have left my course. I did my work there, kept my head down, soon realising that there was so much more to life, so I went on the hunt for a new job!

There she is! I found it, the job that sounded like the dream; a great salary, Monday to Friday, so I could enjoy my weekends, and it was talking to people all day every day! So, I hit the apply button, made my first CV and got myself an interview. I felt confident! I knew in my gut that I would be good at this job, even if I was only eighteen years of age; I was adamant I could do really well. The interview came, yes, I was nervous, but my instinct made my confidence shine, until it got to the part where I had to label the cities on a map of the UK! This was my most painful limiting belief, that I was stupid. Although I wasn't academic, and I had taken no interest in geography, I knew that this was something that I could focus on and learn! Anyway, I left the interview and waited to hear. To say I felt embarrassed would be an understatement! I felt unworthy, stupid, confused and I went home and stayed in my room for a few days, questioning if I would actually be any good at anything! The phone rang, I felt excited, I thought they would see my potential for speaking to customers and would give me the chance to show them my abilities.

'Hi, can I speak with Jenna please?"

'Yes, that's me.'

'Hi Jenna, it's Kelly Anne, I am calling about your recent interview. Unfortunately, you have not been successful this time round.'

My heart sank, my first feeling and experience of rejection and another reason to tell myself that I was stupid and that I would never be great in a job! I knew the reason I didn't get this job was because I didn't have the best geographical knowledge! But I knew I could change this!

After a few days of feeling sorry for myself, I knew that this job was something that I wanted, I knew I would be great at speaking to people and I knew that I could learn everything that was required for me to do the job well. So, I picked up the phone, at the age of eighteen, and asked for another interview!

After a few days, I received an email: "Apologies, Jenna, we have now filled all of the positions and no longer require any more staff." I wasn't prepared to let this go.

In the meantime, I was still stacking shelves. I hated getting up in the morning knowing that I was going to a job that I didn't love. I would snooze my alarm, I would dread the journey, I would think of excuses for why I couldn't go in that day. I just didn't have the energy to be in a job that didn't serve me. From being around my mum, who loved her job, a job that didn't feel like work, I knew there was more out there for me and that feeling this way I had to step out of my comfort zone, start believing in myself again and change what wasn't right! My job! You see, from being a little girl, I was always strong-headed when it came to my gut instinct and going with what felt right. My job didn't feel right, it didn't serve me or make me happy; in fact, it made me miserable. And life is too short to spend more than half of it in a job that contributes to this unhappiness.

A few months down the line, I noticed an advert in the paper again – my dream job (well at that time in my life; I had many dream jobs as the years went on, but we will talk about that later on). Second interview here I come! Boom – this was my chance to go back to the company that rejected me and show them exactly what I had to offer. I polished up on the geography and applied for the same job again, this time with a happy ending! Lesson one learned: Never give up on a dream!

I was at this job for three years, with a promotion in between, before I got itchy feet! That feeling started entering my gut again: I'm bored, I need more, this doesn't challenge me. So, I went on the hunt to find another 'dream job'. My job had been my security and stability for a long time and I didn't realise the rocky road I had ahead of me when I left.

After leaving, I landed myself some amazing 'dream jobs', recruitment, PA, manager, estate agent, sales executive, but I could never settle! I even moved to Spain as a singer for three months and came back after six weeks! I could never hold down a job long enough and the feelings soon started to follow. I got a job, I was ecstatic, I learnt the role, I did really well, I got bored, fed up and applied for another job, got it, was excited and the pattern began! One thing I never did was leave a job without another one secured! This I knew I had to do!

People said I changed jobs like the wind. People would laugh at me; it became a standing joke that no one could keep up with me and with some concern they would try and tell me that this was not normal and that I needed to stay in a job even if I wasn't happy.

This to me was outrageous! Battling with the feelings of guilt, embarrassment, unworthiness and second guessing myself, my gut and instinct still knew that I needed to take this rocky path to get to the one that I have worked hard for now! Even though people's opinions were hurtful and made me believe that what I was doing wasn't right, that I would never get anywhere by not settling in a job, I still found the strength to not allow these thoughts and feelings to influence my path.

I soon discovered that actually, yes, I may have had lots of jobs on my CV with not much commitment to any of them, but I soon felt confident every time I was asked, 'So why did you leave this job?' My answer was always, 'I feel that I have gained so much experience from my previous jobs, sir, with many transferrable skills to this position.'

At this point, I decided that being employed wasn't for me! I knew I wanted to earn a good living to look after me and my mum, to give us a better life and for me to have a life I always dreamed of with no financial worries. I knew I wasn't scared of hard work, but I also wanted to have time freedom. I knew there was something out there for me, but I just hadn't found out what, and my path hadn't been mapped out at this point. I had financial commitments and so I couldn't just leave a job and start a business! Plus, what would I start a business in?! My mind was a whirlwind and actually that is now my nickname, but I love this nickname. As I've grown older and wiser, I now understand why my intuition led me down the difficult path I walked and without it I would never be in the position I am in now.

I used to say to people, 'I know I will be successful one day, I'm just not sure what in yet,' and I truly believed this with every inch and bone of my body! Success to me didn't mean lots of money, success meant that I would help people, guide people to the right paths, have time freedom, collect my children from school, have time off without asking for it and I knew that success was at the end of the journey I was on.

I always held a full-time job and, around the age of twenty-two, I decided to do some short beauty courses and soon qualified in nails and lash lifts. I set up my own business as a mobile beauty therapist and worked in the evenings and weekends to meet my needs of running my own business and, for a while, this made my day job easier as I knew I had something to look forward to after a boring mundane day!

When I was at the age of thirty, I was pregnant with my little boy Luca. This gave me the push to go self-employed. Soon to be a new mummy, I knew now was the time to start my own business. I felt worried, scared and anxious, but I put my all into it, knowing that I wanted to have more time freedom to be a mummy but still earn a living! This was now my time!

After years of rejection, hurt, feeling lost and being laughed at, I now own three businesses, turning over six figures, and they have all made it through a pandemic! I am privileged to help people start their own business in the permanent make up, aesthetics or beauty industry and I coach and mentor those already in the industry who need support and guidance with their business, sales and marketing strategies!

I can now finally say that I have my absolute dream job and my financial freedom is priceless! It took time, life lessons, tears, lots of guts, but I did it! I followed my gut, my heart and my instinct and I created the path I dreamed of!

I never gave up! I wanted to, trust me, there were some days where I looked back on the job websites thinking it would be easier to have a nine-to-five job with no financial worries of when the next bit of business was coming in, but I didn't and I'm glad I didn't! I now celebrate the fact that I have stuck to something for more than a few months, years even! Even today I still believe that my destiny is mapped out and the universe will guide me to where I belong.

My advice to you is that if you have fallen into an industry, job or profession that is not making you happy, then please know that it is possible to find something that you enjoy and love to do whilst making money at the same time. You just need to map out the roads ahead until you reach your destination.

I want my chapter to show the world that being stuck in a rut of unhappiness isn't making the most out of this one precious life that we have! If you have a gut feeling, then stick with it. If people have an opinion then listen but don't let that opinion decide your destiny!

★★★

You can find Jenna here:

Websites – www.jlmentor.co.uk
www.jennaleightrainingacademy.co.uk
FB – https://www.facebook.com/jenna.woodward.31
Instagram – @jennaleighmentor

# BLOOM
## Sharon Highley

*This is for Kass and Alisha – my children who are my absolute world and inspiration. Having you two and being a single mum has taught me some tough lessons, but I believe we are all stronger for those lessons!*

*You both give me a reason to never lose hope, to stay positive and always believe we will come out the other side stronger! Through cancer, relationship breakdowns, terrorist attacks, exams and losing loved ones, we have stuck together and helped each other get through. We've shared amazing, happy times when we've laughed so hard that we've cried and, above all, we've made everlasting memories to treasure forever.*

*My love for you both is bottomless and everlasting and although you are both now adults you will always be my focus and passion in life. I will always be there for you and love you unconditionally.*

*Nothing makes me prouder in life than being your mum. I love you xxxx*

I sat with my head in my hands and tears rolling down my face and all I could think was 'why me?'

It was the first Christmas with my baby son. I had been with my partner a few years and we had a good relationship, I thought, until I found out he was having an affair. My world fell apart and I was devasted. I was desperately sad and one day walked out of work mid-shift and just drove. Without realising what I was doing, I sent messages to my mum and friend telling them to make sure my son knew I always loved him. I turned my phone off and walked. I walked and walked and walked with no idea where I was going. Hours and hours later, something snapped in my head and I knew my son needed me. I made my way back to the car to find countless messages from family and friends upset and worried about me. I realised I was loved, wanted and cherished by so many people, so why had I only been listening to the voice of one – the one who didn't value me at all?

Despite this and the mental abuse I was so used to by now, I wanted to be a family so much and we sorted things out, got back together and seemed to get back on track.

Fast forward two years and I'd just had my daughter, who was five weeks old, and it was Christmas again. I thought I had everything I could possibly want as I sat there on Christmas Eve. An argument about something and nothing turned nasty and taking my two children (both under three) from their beds, along with all their presents laid out so beautifully in the lounge, I left and drove to my mum's. When I arrived, it was 12.50am – Christmas Day was here!

That night was the start of a massive shift in my way of thinking and, although I didn't realise it then, I had hit rock bottom and the only way was up! The months that followed were some of the hardest times I had experienced so far in my life. I had been mentally abused for years in this relationship without really realising it was happening. I felt so sad, unloved and useless.

I was working as a full-time paramedic doing twelve-hour day and night shifts and I had two children under three. My parents and extended family were amazing and looked after my children while I worked, and I looked after them while I was home. I sold the house I had bought with my partner and bought my first house on my own. I was so proud of myself for pulling myself up out of the mess I was in to build a future for me and my children. However, I craved the family scene. With most of my friends happily married with children and the 'ideal' life, I felt I was missing out and, more importantly, I was worried my children were too. So, I took him back and let him move in with us. The relationship progressed but it didn't take long for me to realise I had made the biggest mistake of my life, but this time I was in control. This was my house and I decided to end things. I packed his bags and he was gone!

The relief I felt that night I can still feel today. I knew without a doubt I had reached the point where I was strong enough to say 'enough' and stop this self-destructive path I kept finding myself back on.

I knew that my children deserved better, that I would never let my children be at a disadvantage because they had a single mum and that I was going to give them everything they could ever want in life. I loved them with an ache deep inside and would bring them up in a happy, secure, loving home making memories. The three of us were a family that nothing or no one would ever destroy!

This is where I felt my life started again. I was a single, working mum and felt I had a lot to prove to myself, my children and the world, but I have never been more sure that I wouldn't just survive but I would thrive!

The children and I spent years as a family of three. Some of my happiest memories are of these times with my children. We went on holidays, days out, weekends away, stayed with friends – we were happy.

My job as a paramedic paid me well and as I worked twelve-hour shifts, it meant I only worked three shifts a week and got full-time pay. It worked very well for me for many, many years. After twenty-five years as a paramedic and with the work getting more and more risky and violent, I came to the decision I needed to leave in 2014. I was constantly thinking if something happens to me my children will be alone, and it played on my mind. So, I started a new job with my paramedic experience but office based. I never enjoyed this like I had being a paramedic and started to feel there must be more to life than this! I lived for my annual leave during school holidays when I could spend time with my children.

In 2016, I was diagnosed with breast cancer – I was

forty-five. Again, I sat with my head in my hands and asked, 'Why me?' The moment I heard the words 'you have cancer' are forever etched in my mind, but the pain in my heart having to tell my children was unbearable. They were fifteen and thirteen, too young to lose their mum, and there was no way I was going to let that happen. They were my rocks through gruelling chemotherapy, radiotherapy and operations and they gave me the determination to get through and keep positive. These were the toughest days of my life but with every part of me I fought to get better, and I was one of the lucky ones who did. My children didn't deserve to see their mum looking like I did or feeling like I did, and I felt guilty that I'd put them through such an awful time when they were at such an impressionable and notoriously hard stage in their lives. My son was sitting his GCSEs and I felt so guilty for being ill when he should have been concentrating on his exams. I couldn't be prouder that he still passed all eleven.

At this point, I should also mention that my daughter and I had been looking forward to seeing a little known (then in the UK) singer. My daughter was a huge fan and was so excited. It turned out I was in hospital having my lymph nodes removed on the day of the concert, so my sister stood in and took my daughter to see the long-awaited concert at the Manchester Arena. The singer was Ariana Grande and the night was 22nd May 2017, the night a suicide bomber set off a bomb and killed twenty-two people. I knew about the explosion from my sister before it hit the news headlines and I will be forever grateful that I knew right from the start they were alive. The relief still brings me to tears almost four years on. My daughter and sister have struggled emotionally ever since. My happy, carefree daughter changed overnight and became scared and anxious and sad about every part of her life. Again, I felt guilty – guilty that I wasn't with her when she needed me the most in her life. The fear of what could have happened when I wasn't with her was overwhelming. It's been a long road to recovery – one she is still struggling with – but I'm so proud of her and the way she copes with what life throws at her. I have learnt that everything happens for a reason and I wasn't meant to be with her that night. Had I been I would have been weak from the chemotherapy I'd just finished and unable to run with her to safety (which at the time was what happened, as they had no idea if there were more bombs or if it was a gunman). I also couldn't have been a support for her emotionally through the aftermath of that night if I was involved and was struggling emotionally myself. So, I believe I was meant to not be there and have learnt to turn the guilt into something positive.

My cancer treatment left me with many side effects, including constant pain, which meant I was unable to return to work. I had only ever been in paramedic roles and now I was faced with being unable to do my job. As a single mum that was a huge worry and I knew that being given a second chance of life I was meant to use it to create something special – something I was proud of and that would make my children proud.

I fell into network marketing after buying a product from a local representative and loving it. The seed was sown that I could make an amazing business all from home. I tried to put the idea out of my head – everyone knows network marketing doesn't make you rich! Right? I couldn't shake the idea, though, and after some research, I signed up. What did I have to lose, as it was free, after all. I'm so happy and grateful I took that chance because now I'm building a successful empire of my very own from home. I have the perfect job in the best location – home.

The events and decisions in my life have moulded the person I am today. I'm the strong, independent, motivated, confident, enthusiastic, positive and life loving person I am today because of all the heartache and pain I've been through. The past shapes the future you and if you are in a low, dark place right now, you have two choices! Either let those events you've been through define you and destroy you, or use them to make you stronger and create something amazing.

My thoughts for you today would be stay strong and never lose sight of who you are! Don't let anyone try to change you, however much you think they care! Someone who wants to change you doesn't love you! Don't ignore your gut feeling! When someone or something is changing you as a person in a bad way and your family or friends tell you, don't ignore them – they know and love you most!

We have to reach rock bottom before we can climb back up and this will happen more than once to most of us in our lives, but always remember you are strong and you can and will rise to become an amazing, strong, focused woman.

Always remember this: When you're in a dark place you tend to think you've been buried but perhaps you've been planted. Go and bloom xxxx

★★★

You can find Sharon here:

Personal Facebook – https://www.facebook.com/sharon.harrop.77
https://instagram.com/savvy_mum_sharon

Parallel Perfumes – https://www.facebook.com/parallelperfumes
https://instagram.com/parallelperfumesbyfmworld

# YOUR INNER LIGHT CAN OUTSHINE ANY THUNDERSTORM

## Clare Edwards

*This chapter is firstly dedicated to my first-born daughter, you are my rock, you are my light, and you are the reason I hung on to hope for all those years.*

*Secondly to my parents, who have picked me up time after time and never ever gave up on me.*

*And finally, to all those who have suffered abuse, feel they are not good enough and have lost hope – may you hear me when I say the light inside you will guide you in the end, hold on, find faith grab my hand. You can do this!*

There was another thunderstorm raging outside my window, the noise was so loud, and the rain was so forceful. I stared out so hard with no idea what I was hoping to find but I knew it was better out there, somewhere, anywhere that was not here.

Here was a place of such darkness, fear, sadness, hurt and loneliness. Here was, of course, deep inside of me and wherever I was or went I was still there in that same place. No storm was going to take me away from it all. I was a broken-hearted, shattered, beaten down, scared little girl. The tears streamed uncontrollably, I opened the window to drown out the noise from within and prayed that this would all end one day. I longed for someone to come and save me from this pain.

Have you ever just sat and stared out of the window, wishing, hoping and praying for something, ANYTHING?

This was slowly becoming something that I was doing almost every day; my life as I knew it had fallen apart. The pain I was put through was breaking me, the strength I had was disappearing and my life was becoming just an existence and one that I did not want to be part of anymore.

The physical scars I had endured were severe, but the mental scars were so much worse. I could not think straight, my anger was at levels I never even knew existed. I was a complete an utter emotional wreck that did not know how to even feel anymore.

I was on this hamster wheel that had become my life and I just could not see the way out. There was only one reason that I kept going every day, regardless of how I was feeling, and that was my first born. She was my hope, she was my light, she was my everything. If I did not have her, God only knows where my life would have ended up.

I always knew I was meant for more; I knew I was meant to help people in life, but I could not even help myself. I could leave and I did many times, but the thoughts, limiting beliefs and doubts had been so far embedded inside of me that I always went back because I felt that was all I deserved and all I was meant to have. I felt this was the only person I could ever love and who could ever love me. I was so angry that I was put through these terrible traumas because I did not want to leave, I did not make that choice, my choice was taken away from me because of the violent episodes and sheer unsafe environment I was in. I had to leave now or possibly lose that chance forever.

So, I now had to give up our beautiful home because I could not afford it on my own, the council would not help me because I was working, I could not rent anywhere else alone because I did not earn enough on paper, I was stuck. The council said I would have to be homeless for them to help me, so I stopped paying the rent and had to endure the court process and eviction so I could get some help. It's messed up really, but that is how it works, unfortunately. If you work and try to support yourself and your family, you get no help.

Eviction day came and it was just me and my daughter with my little car. We had been given a one-bedroom third-floor self-contained flat. I was so sad, I was tired, I was exhausted, I was emotionally drained, but I packed up and made umpteen trips to the new place, lugging everything up three flights of stairs with my daughter begrudgingly helping me. It was the longest, most painful day. I sorted her room out and made it as comfortable as I could with what we could take and then I had the lounge/kitchen as my bedroom.

I was back at the window, sobbing silently all night, thinking how am I back in this place again? What have I done so bad to deserve this life? Will I ever be happy and free?

Life was just messy from this point; I was drinking pretty much daily and my drug taking was only contributing to the way I was feeling. It stopped the hurt for that short amount of time but then *bam* it would smack me in the face so much harder the next day. Along with all the anger, fear, hurt and pain, now came anxiety, guilt and shame.

I went on like this for some time, a few jobs, scraping by, letting other people come into my space and cause me problems. I was mixing with all the wrong people and I had just given up on my life. My beautiful little girl's behaviour had changed so much, and I knew it was because of what I was subjecting her to, and then came more guilt, more shame. I knew something had to change before I ruined her life like I was ruining mine.

I stopped mixing with the wrong people and was trying to get my life in some sort of order. I had got a decent job as a supervisor. I stopped the drinking and started going to the gym and, even though I was not happy, I was on my way to maybe getting there one day. I met someone new and that developed quickly but started as friends. It was this relationship that stopped me from letting that person back into my life to rip it apart again. It had been fourteen years and it was only now when I said I would never go back that I meant it.

Due to all the wrong people I had been around, the

noise I had apparently made in my flat previously had caused people to complain about me and I was being threatened with yet another eviction. I tried to fight it, but I knew something bad was coming, I could feel it in my gut.

I came home from work one day to our temporary accommodation only to find the eviction papers taped to the door and the locks changed.

It was that moment I knew it was about to become the darkest days I had been through yet and I was not wrong. I had to pick my girl up from school and go to social services for help. I was made to feel the worst mother going, I was told I had made myself intentionally homeless and they did not have to help me. I was told they had the obligation to house my daughter and would do that without me. Basically, they'd take her away from me, my life, my reason to breathe. I was a mess. I begged, I pleaded, no one understood what was going on in my head, no one understood the damage I had endured, no one was listening, my life was ending right in front of my eyes.

I wanted to grab my little girl and run as fast as I could, but I had nothing, nowhere to go, no money. This was the end...

Or so I thought. But after months of stress, meetings, hotel rooms, temporary rooms in houses full of people I did not know, my daughter not wanting to be with me at these places, many nights of crying myself to sleep, sick every day with anxiety and worry, it happened...

I found a place that I could privately rent, I had managed

to have my job kept open while we were moving around from place to place, and they were going to accept me as a tenant with part income and part benefits. I was saved, this was my chance to make things different and my chance to never ever let us go through any of this again.

My daughter was happier, we moved into our new home and began to put things back to some sort of normality. I made a solemn promise to never return to that toxic relationship EVER again and that was nearly four years ago.

I had so many triggers from my past that I was still living in a life of anger, upset, doubt, existence, without knowing my own true self, although I did not realise this. I could not work out why I was not genuinely happy when I had what I thought I had always wanted.

Why was I so angry all the time?

Why did I blame my partner for everything?

Why were my emotions so up and down all the time?

So, the years of mental abuse had created this whole other person, so defensive towards everything and everyone, never feeling happy, non-trusting and thinking that everyone wanted to hurt me, that I was not entitled to have a happy ending, that my life had been ruined and I was so bitter.

I fell pregnant and then I had a reason for my emotional weaknesses, or so I told myself, this was why I was all over the place. Well, that lasted for the nine months and then I was blessed with my second beautiful daughter. I moved to a better, bigger house and life was good... Or was it?

So, while at home on maternity leave, I started to think about my life and what I wanted for my future. I did not want to go back to work in my office job nine-to-five, and I did not want to put my little girl in childcare to do this either. I knew I was never going to get that dream life I started to think about, and I was never going to be financially abundant, and I was sick of struggling.

I was overweight at this point, and really struggling with my own self-esteem and emotions were rocky to say the least. I was searching online for random things, as you do, and I came across an advert about some weight loss shakes by a celebrity I had watched on TV. So, I bit the bullet and decided I needed to sort me out so I could be more confident and clearer headed to decide what I was going to do next. It was this that led me to find an opportunity to work from home and it was called network marketing, something I had never heard of before. So basically, I would tell people about these products I was using, and I could earn money from it. My thoughts were, 'What have I got to lose? If I start now and it works, I might not have to return to my office job,' and that was the goal.

This network marketing thing was like nothing before. I was told to copy the successful people, I was told you need to tell 'your story'. I was told you need to do personal development every day (what the hell is personal development, I wondered).

So, I started to copy the successful people, I was getting books, listening to motivational podcasts and trying to take in all the training that I possibly could. I got very overwhelmed, doubts crept in and I questioned is this even for me. I soon realised that I was not really into the health and fitness thing, I just wanted to lose weight and that I did, so I decided this was not for me anymore.

I had decided that I loved this idea of working from home and it seemed that there were a lot of different companies that offered this. I found one that was about coffee. Now, I love coffee, you did not have to be in tip top shape to fit in either, so I tried it. I was not successful, and I just could not get into the swing of things. I did not know why or what the problem was, but I was not getting anywhere. The more I was told to just be yourself, the more I closed up and the less I did. What the hell was wrong with me now? This just was not right for me either. I did ask myself if I was passionate about the products and the answer was no, I just knew that I liked coffee initially.

By this point my maternity leave was getting closer to the end and I was getting more and more worried about what I was going to do with my life. I was not happy and felt I was still in that place of just floating through life. This was not the end, though, and I knew there was something out there for me. I knew that if I could just find the right company with the right products that this was the career choice for me, and I would be able to help so many other women just like me.

I researched and started to think of the things that I liked, and I eventually found the right company to really get this thing off the ground for me. I had joined the super attractor academy and was learning all things mindset and manifestation and how to be a super attractor online.

All these things were foreign to me, but it was a welcome distraction and it felt good to be doing something for myself for once. So, there I was, putting all this into action, but I was really struggling with this whole 'my story' part. But mostly I was struggling with the fact that I was told to find groups about your hobbies and interests and build connections with these like-minded people. All amazing advice but... who even was I? I did not even know what I liked anymore, so many years of being told how to act, what to do, who to be, and doing things that I did not want to do, I did not even know what I did want to do anymore.

I needed more help, a much deeper help. I got one-to-one coaching with JoJo and began this incredible healing journey. With timeline therapy work, we dug deep into all my negative emotions and beliefs. I cannot even put into words how incredibly relieved I felt to finally realise that my life spiralling the way it did was due to all the things I was made to believe and feel. My whole identity had been stripped and I was so goddamn lost. Slowly we released anger, followed by fear, guilt, sadness, and so much more along the way. Each day, each week, I would feel lighter, see things more clearly, feel differently about things. This was the most powerful thing I have ever experienced; my life is changing every day for the better and it feels incredible.

When I look out of the window now it's only to see

what the weather is like and to decide what I want to do that day. Even though my journey is only just beginning, I clearly see the vision and it excites me. I know my worth and I am now finding me again. I have become more in touch with my spiritual side and calm has surrounded me. I am learning more about meditation, crystals, the divine and practising grounding and staying tuned into my emotions and what is going on around me.

I have now started to build a very fast-growing team, I deliver trainings in my own training group, I give value and support and I am there to show others that it does not matter what you have been through or what you have held onto, you can let go and have the life you deserve.

I have hit my biggest promotion to date, I have received my biggest commissions to date and I now have the strength, the knowledge, the emotional intelligence and pure desire to want to help others, and now finally I have 'my story'.

So, if you are out there reading this chapter and you are somebody who is feeling lost or are unsure of where their life is heading right now, trust me when I tell you the light inside you is brighter than you can ever imagine and you are worthy of having everything you desire.

If you have a dream, then you can absolutely go out there and achieve that, all you need to do is have faith in you like I do. If I can go through the absolute worst that I have and come out the other side in the way that I have then you absolutely can too. It is your birth right to live in happiness and abundance.

★★★

You can find Clare here:

www.ultimatelyu.co.uk
Clare@ultimatelyu.co.uk
https://linktr.ee/UltimatelyU

# YOUR STRUGGLES CAN BECOME YOUR STRENGTHS

## Rachel Raines

*This is a chapter dedicated to anyone who has ever suffered loss or struggled in any given area of life. I want you to know it's okay to hurt, but it's also okay to move forward. Speak up, don't stay silent and don't stay stuck. Turn those struggles into something powerful, I believe in you.*

It was the middle of the night on the 30th of November 2010, the phone rang, panic hit, 'you must come now'. The smell, I remember the smell, the cold air and the fluffy snow that covered the ground that morning. The road was slippy, mustn't drive fast, but all I wanted him to do was to put his foot down and accelerate to a hundred miles an hour. The drive was the longest thirty minutes of my life. We made our way down the well-lit corridor, which somehow seemed dark, sad, empty and cold. My body, my body felt numb, no emotion, just empty. I knew what was about to happen.

The nurse hugged us with tears and pain in her eyes. 'I'm sorry but he's gone.' The next five hours I spent staring at him, hoping he would move and praying to God, who I didn't believe in until that moment, to just bring him back.

That moment was the very moment in time when my world crumbled into a million pieces, the moment I lost all control. My protector, my best friend, the man who always knew the right thing to say, the man who always had a smile and a positive spin on every situation. My dad was gone.

The days passed, the weeks turned to months and then to years. Time seemed to stand still for me but still move for everyone else, I had allowed myself not to feel, to lock away any ounce of emotion to protect myself; if you don't feel, you don't hurt was my thinking, but how wrong was I? Never dealing with the pain brought me to some deep and extremely dark places.

Depression, anxiety, the signs were there, but I found a way to hide it from the world. From the outside I was smiling, on the inside I was drowning. Cancelling plans became a normal thing that was the first sign. My friendship circle slowly became smaller and smaller; who wants a friend that cancels plans ten times in a row, right?

My life became reliant on mainly one thing: food. Food was my comfort, it made me feel good if only for a minute; it was my lifeline. The jeans started to get tighter, my body started to change, from a healthy lean body came rolls and stretch marks that I had never had before.

As the weight came on fast, so did the anxiety, the excuses became more frequent, my whole life became reliant on eating. I never really realised at the time that there was a problem, I lived in a state of darkness for so long that it just started to become normal; this was how my life would be, I suppose, so I'll just eat my way through it, food feels good.

Then it got worse. Leaving the house in the middle of winter and breaking out in a sweat is not usually a thing, but it was for me daily, the sweat soaking through my clothes, running down my neck and leaving my hair looking like I'd just left the house after taking a shower. Walking past people, getting even hotter, working myself up at the thought they were staring at me, the heart palpitations and my favourite one, the feeling that you're going to shit yourself the minute you leave the house, yep that's anxiety, full blown I'm going to shit my pants in public or on this bus. I'll clear it up now, I never shit myself, but it came close. I spent almost eight years of my life stuck in the same routine, never moving forward and all the above feelings just became the normal day-to-day things in my world.

The struggles continued, things became strained with Dean. From meeting at fourteen, falling head-over-heels in love with him on a family holiday in Turkey, it seemed like a fairy tale from the outside, but behind closed doors it all started to fall apart.

The years went on and I fell pregnant with my first child, my beautiful Mia. There came some pretty dark moments that I've never spoken about, to this day this will be the first time I've fully opened up about these thoughts. What if? What if the pain could just go away, would Dean and Mia be better off without a partner and a mother who struggled to even leave the house, a partner and mother who had amounted to nothing and – how I saw it at the time – achieved absolutely nothing with her life? I had become distant, I lost feelings for the ones I loved the most. Dean had his own struggles, and the day came when it all became too much and he moved out.

In a dark place, with a child who just didn't understand why mummy and daddy argued and why daddy didn't come home, I had lost all control. My eating started again, my mind started to crumble, I had lost my partner, my dad and my identity; I didn't know who I was anymore.

A moment of weakness, just one tiny time. Just in case you didn't know, you can get pregnant from having sex once and using the pulling out method – just a heads up for all you ladies reading this, you're welcome. It happened, pregnant, oh fuck. Financially I was in the worst position of my life, mentally in a pretty dark place, and the only light I had at that time was my ray of sunshine, Mia. Could I be a single mum to two children? How would this pan out, what if we didn't work things out, how would I do this alone?

I lost count of how many people told me to terminate the pregnancy, but my instinct told me I just couldn't: trust your gut, listen to yourself, your intuition is usually spot on. I created life and I'd already lost so much, I would fix things, not just for me but for my babies.

There's blood, so much blood, the screaming, oh my God, Mum, there's blood. The journey, the same feeling as the feeling I had seven years prior, just numb, I expected the worst.

The feeling of loss is something most of us have to experience, but we are never ready for it. The feeling sticks with you, it imprints on you forever. Sliding the ultrasound over my tummy, it's good news and bad news: the baby is okay, however you have a tear in your uterus just above the baby. There's a chance it could heal or a chance it could get worse, you need to take it easy. Well, that's easier said than done with a three-year-old running riot. But the relief and feeling I had, I instantly knew I had made the right choice. I would do all I could to protect this baby.

I'm a strong believer now that sometimes things do happen for a reason; maybe my dad was meant for greater, more powerful things. Who knows until it's our time? But I now believe that getting pregnant happened for a reason. I suppose, in a way, I could say that my children saved me. They kept me going. Over the next few months, things changed. Dean had a breakthrough, he came home after having struggles of his own, but that's his story to share, not mine. Things started to get better, I felt loved, protected and the feeling of darkness lifted slightly; there was light at the end of the tunnel, I could see it. The months passed, my tummy grew, life at home got better, and our relationship seemed to grow stronger. Days out became more frequent, leaving the house was a little less scary at one point. I would say the hardest times were when I was alone, my thoughts overpowering reality, the negative self-talk, that was all still very real.

He arrived on the 21st of July 2017, our Joshua. He was perfect in every way. Life was good. What brings more joy than a bundle of light? Mia's love for her baby brother was something I hope you all get to see, I'll never forget her smile when we brought him home, memories that will last a lifetime. Our perfect family was complete.

Things seemed to settle, life became somewhat normal, I returned to work after maternity leave, but the feelings I'd held in for so long started to creep again to the surface. The eating began, the anxiety creeped back in and I found myself becoming the biggest I'd ever been, a size 24 and almost 19 stone. Life again became a struggle, the simplest things were exhausting. Why did I feel this way? Two beautiful children, a partner that loved me, why was this darkness taking over again?

Going to work became hard, the feeling of dread, I hated every aspect of going to work, the excuses started, I lost my job, and that was it, our financial stability was gone in an instant.

Breaking point came when a full-length picture was posted of me on social media. My worst fear, everyone could now see what I had become. What had I done, why had I done this to myself? I had self-sabotaged in every aspect of my life, who even was I? It hit me, my anxiety, the reason I felt this way, it was who I had let myself become, the fear of people seeing me. I'd gone from an outgoing, happy, care-free girl, to a morbidly obese, exhausted, depressed and anxious mess; this wasn't me, it wasn't who I wanted to be anymore.

It takes a lot to put your hands up, to admit to yourself that you have control of who you are and who you become. Everything I had become was all from my own choices. I had spent eight years of my life playing the victim, playing the blame game, when in fact it was all on me. I self-sabotaged, I closed myself off, I blamed the world for my problems, but it was all on me to change.

They say that something as small as the flutter of a butterfly's wings can cause a typhoon halfway across the world. I had let those small things cause a typhoon in my mind. Every negative thought, every crumb that entered my mouth, it created a monster of a typhoon.

There always comes a time for change, but how, where to start? I don't know why, I don't know how, but I pressed the live button on social media and eight years of emotion came flooding out onto everyone's screens; maybe I was trying to explain the picture? Maybe it was to finally release in order to move on? I honestly can't remember, but I finally, after eight long years, opened up.

Talking does not make us weak, opening up is a strength. Find the courage to speak up, I promise the weight lifted is worth every ounce of courage it takes.

No identity, no qualifications, made redundant three times, anxiety, depression, morbidly obese, where to start in fixing all these obstacles?

I'd dabbled in network marketing and online businesses over the years but never really had any success. It seemed a lot of companies I joined I paid more in than I got out, but something caught my eye and pulled me back. Are you stuck? Are you exhausted? Are you eating too much? Do you have brain fog? Well, I ticked every one of those boxes. What is this, let me give that a try, what did I have to lose? This moment changed every aspect of my life from the moment I decided to just be opened-minded and give it a go.

I fell in love, instantly, the feeling I got, it was all about the feeling. I felt good and that to me was priceless. The weight started to fall off, my clothes started to loosen, my mood lifted, I started to open up, my confidence slowly started to shine brighter and brighter. After having made mistakes in the past, and having failed ventures, I learned one of the most important key points is to fall in love with what you're promoting. It may not be for everyone, but if it's for you and you have the passion, you're always going to find those people who align with you, the company and also the product. I became obsessed, in a good way, having results became addictive. Then it hit, okay what if I could help others? I love it, others will too.

What is meant for you will always find you. Sometimes we mistake opportunity as hard work, or we mistake it as a pyramid because your Uncle Nobhead told you it's illegal. I'm here to tell you to take that risk, don't hold back out of fear, don't hold back because of the opinions of others. Other people's opinions do not define you, you define you, your life, your rules and your choices. What happened for me after this moment really changed me and my whole world for the better.

Someone asked me, what's your why? Anyone in networking hear that a lot? My why, what on earth do you mean my why, I see so many people with confused faces wondering what I'm talking about when they first join my team. I was told back then that if your why doesn't make you cry it isn't strong enough and I fully stand by that statement.

My why stems from everything you've just read. Yes, I needed more money, yes, I needed better health, yes, I needed to find me. But it didn't make me cry, I had to dig deeper.

So, let's revisit my dad. My dad had a heart of gold, his smile could light up a room. Growing up, I had the most amazing childhood, I never wanted for anything, but this came at a price and that price was my parents' time.

To provide, they had to work long hours, my dad working four jobs at a time at one point, I don't think he was ever at home during the last years of his life, which must have been super stressful, right? I know one job is stressful, let alone four jobs.

At just forty-eight, he suffered a heart attack and then went on to suffer a fatal stroke at just fifty-two, one day after my twenty-first birthday, which sadly ended his life.

My why took me a while to find, but when I looked at how hard my mum and dad both worked, I realised my why was time-freedom, not just for me but for my partner. To be able to work flexibly, without financial worry and to live life on our terms. What other job could I get that could potentially give me the above, apart from the industry I'm a part of right now? I'll wait… None, right? Unless I wanted to get into the adult film industry, but to be honest, I don't think Dean would be down for that.

Not only do I want time-freedom, but I've found a love for helping others, showing people how to create something they never thought possible. That does something to me, seeing others achieve, that's the feeling that gets me each and every day. People like me and you, people who have come from struggle and achieved amazing things. My why drives me to do better, to be better, and to show others what's possible when you finally start to believe in you.

From the girl stuck, with no vision and no way out, to now a girl who has a purpose, a direction, a happy and healthy mind, and to think it all started by just saying I'll give this a go.

You're wanting to grow a successful business online? You're wanting more? My advice to you: Be coachable, never stop learning, never stop growing.

Always be you, share your struggles, that's okay, people relate to real people. Don't 'fake it till you make it', that shit gets boring and from experience you can't keep up a false image, people see straight through it. Surround yourself with winners, people who want you to succeed.

Release any negative hidden emotions, you can't grow if your mind holds you back, you will become stuck.

Connect to your why, it needs to be the very reason you get up in the morning.

You will have hard days, you will feel like giving up, power through those days, show up even when you don't feel like it, these days bring growth and lead you to the greatest days.

Focus on helping others. Always remember that you do not need people, you can want people on your team or as your customer, but you do not need them, there is a difference. If you're passionate and genuine, the right people will align with you. Who can you help? Focus on helping not needing! People need your help.

For everyone who is reading this and has suffered loss, heartache, depression, anxiety, I beg you to speak up, take action, only you can progress forward. Only when I released did I start to blossom.

100lbs lost in weight, a thriving online business, a happy and healthy mind, a fiancé Dean who loves and adores me and me him, two beautiful happy children who I get to spend as much time with as I like.

Your happy ending is waiting for you, just have the courage to pursue it. I still have a long way to go to get to where I want to be, but each day brings me closer, my vision is now crystal clear.

Success to me isn't just an income, it's a mindset. Success is growth, success is finding who you are, finally believing in yourself and becoming the person who you want to be. The power of success all lies with you. I'm no one special, I'm just the girl who never gave up.

I made my dad proud. Who knows if he's watching, but if he is, I know he's smiling and saying keep going princess you're doing it. They are always with you, remember the happy times, stay strong, better times await you. Let your struggles now become your strengths.

★★★

You can find Rachel Here:

https://www.facebook.com/rachel.raines.543
www.Instagram.com/Rachel.raines
https://vm.tiktok.com/ZMeyKfTG6/

# Don't Stay Stuck, You Really Don't Have to. Life Is Short, Do What Your Heart Desires

## Rachel Doyle

*I want to dedicate this chapter to my da, thank you for being my hero and for showing kindness in life to me and to other people, you had a heart of gold, I will love you always and am forever grateful for the fourteen years I spent with you.*

*I also want to thank my uncle Colm, who stepped in and kept his promise to my da to look after me, and my ma, who has shown me how to be resilient and not to give up on my dreams.*

*My nan was also a big supporter in my life and I will never forget her words to me, "You only get one crack at it." Nanny, I hope I am making you proud.*

My name is Rachel Doyle and I want to share my story with you and I hope that this can inspire people to do what they want to do in life.

I grew up in a council estate in Dublin. It wasn't easy and the worst time of my life was when I was fourteen. I was out drinking with my friends one night and I snuck off to walk home.

A few minutes away from my house, I was vulnerable and in a state from the amount of vodka I had consumed. I was raped that night and up until this day I don't know by who.

I remember it down to a tee, and when I woke up the next morning it all felt so surreal, I tried to put it to the back of my head. When my family found out, they were distraught. The police didn't treat me fairly as I was drunk, so that made me lack belief in the justice system. Two weeks later, my life took another shit turn.

It was 9th of June and I remember it like it was yesterday. It was a hot day and I was planning on having a few drinks with my friends. My ma called me and asked me to come home as she had to tell me something. I got to my house and my uncle Colm and my da's best friend were there too. My ma was crying and she grabbed my hand. Her very words were, "Rachel, your da has passed away, love."

I grabbed my hand back and said, "Ma, he can't be gone!" With that, I ran from my house crying my eyes out.

My world had fallen apart in less than thirty days and I was fourteen!

For months after my da's death, I went through a shit time in school, missing days, smoking, drinking anything to try and block out what was going on. I even went to counselling, and that worked for a while, but I had completely blocked out the rape, as the death of my dad had put it to the back of my head.

I tried to make sure my family were always okay and looking after others did take me away from the real shit that I was going through deep down.

I hated school, never wanted to be there, but I finished anyway, as it was what my ma and da wanted for me.

I didn't go to college as I have the gift of the gab, so I worked in restaurants and sales jobs.

Around five years ago was the turning point for me in my life!

I'd lost my dad and watched my mother beat breast cancer and I just thought to myself, "Fuck this shit! We get one life, why am I not taking a chance and doing something better for myself?"

One day out of the blue, I said, "Ma, I'm moving to Manchester and I'm going to do something with my life." She was delighted for me. I came to the UK on the 2nd of January 2018. I left my comfort zone where I had grown up and leaving my niece and nephews was especially hard, but I wanted to make sure their auntie could buy them some extra nice pressies too.

I arrived in Manchester with my massive pink suitcase. The zip ended up breaking and I had to wrap it with lots of yellow tape, a nightmare, just my luck.

I got a job in recruitment in the engineering sector. I loved it and for a while my life was so random, meeting new people and I felt free.

My ma's breast cancer came back and I had to go back home to see her. Thankfully she got through it again, she's as strong as an ox, and I randomly decided to leave my job and move to Preston, as I'd started to feel "stuck" again.

I moved into a house share and got a nine-to-five job in sales for the time being. I also met someone and got into a relationship. I was vulnerable, in a way, and as the months went on, I realised this person was toxic and I had to get out and value myself more.

I also started to feel like I was lacking something in my job again. I remember one day I just left and for a while I felt like a free spirit.

I kept saying to myself that the next time I met someone they had to be a good man, preferably someone who worked in construction, as I loved the outfit, and low and behold I met my partner one evening when I went for a drink and, immediately, I knew he was for me.

Again, I got a job in a sales office and I did fall in love with the product. I was making good money and I loved the people like my family.

I made myself a vision board and everything I put on it, such as travel, money, a family, success, etc., made me get excited, but putting a nine-to-five up there didn't move me.

I started to feel really bored and it was like a burning desire in me. I started to look into what it would be like to be my own boss and the more I did I got scared of the idea of leaving my comfort zone but I knew I had it in me deep down to be someone other than an average Jo at a desk, I have the personality to do more.

I knew I had to work on my own personal development in order to be successful, as I often compared my own journey to someone else's and was so hard on myself to the point where it made me feel mentally exhausted.

I found the Femalepreneur Academy and I decided to jump in and join, which really helped. I then decided to do some more inner work and sign up for one-to-one sessions with Natasha.

I worked on my mindset and started to manifest things that I wanted, and I felt like I was being guided to what I was supposed to be doing. I do think my da is helping me.

I wished I had done it sooner, as I healed wounds and limiting beliefs from my childhood and also started to love myself more and realised I can be who the fuck I want to be because I have put a lot of negative shit to bed.

I finally have some clarity on my life now, I know I want to be a successful businesswoman and I want to be the boss of my own life. I am making plans for my future with my partner, and I want to be the best version of myself in every way possible.

My overall message to the people reading this: Don't stay stuck in a job you hate, a relationship you don't want to be in, you deserve more, so ask for it, there is better out there. Believe in yourself! You are meant to do more than just average.

My da's death was the worst thing that happened to me but it also made me the person I am today. I am stronger and I will push to get to where I want to be.

★★★

You can find Rachel here:

https://www.facebook.com/rachel.doyle.33821189
www.instagram.com/blush_scents

# FROM ROCK BOTTOM TO RESILIENCE

## Claire Lowe

*This chapter is dedicated to my three children Maisie-Anne, Sofia and Joshua. You are the light in my life and my reason why. You have helped me more than you could know, I'm so proud of you. You have faced many challenges and adversities in your life but have grown up to be strong, confident , kind and resilient. I love you x*

*To anyone reading this who can relate to my story, either in their personal life or business, my message to you is to be brave, be confident to make a change, believe in you, be you. You are worthy and deserve the best in all aspects of your life.*

I was born into a loving family that always wanted the best for me and had strong values, which gave me a great foundation for my life. My father was a language teacher, and we were able to enjoy family holidays abroad, often visiting the places he had been to on his school trips. I have happy memories of our camping holidays as a family with my brothers, which instilled my love for travel and other cultures. I went on to train as a nurse and, through this, I gained an interest in complementary therapies and the health and well-being benefits of them. I pursued my interest and took a course in Holistic Aromatherapy at the prestigious Tisserand Institute in London. After which, I set up my own mobile business and worked this part time around my nursing. I loved seeing the benefits of how my therapeutic treatments helped people. I didn't think so at that time but on reflection this was the start of my entrepreneurial journey.

In my twenties, I had a few relationships, which weren't the best for me at that time and sadly I had a couple of miscarriages along the way, which were my first experience of loss. Eventually, my life led me to my future husband who made me smile and laugh and we welcomed our first child into the world.

My early married life was happy, and I was blessed with two more children. However, a few years later, our family had a traumatic loss, which then led to addictive behaviour as a way of numbing grief. Alcohol was turned to, to numb the pain. Over the years, I was surrounded by the energy of arguments, stress and inappropriate language being aimed at me. I had to find a way out as I didn't want my children being within this environment.

I want you to understand when you are living your life in the midst of it, you can feel trapped. I had often come close to leaving over the years, but something always stopped me – that was fear. Fear of being alone, fear of not being able to cope financially for myself and my children. Through the years, my self-esteem and self-worth had been stripped from me. I felt alone, and I was lonely in my own head. To the outside world, I was a positive and bubbly person, always smiling. This was a front as behind my smile and inside of me I was crying. I had completely lost myself; I was living on autopilot. I was depressed, often going to bed at night crying silent tears into my pillow. Deep down, I knew that I had to break out, and I felt a deep sadness inside of me. I had carried a lot of guilt inside of me and blamed myself for not leaving sooner. However, one of the biggest lessons I have learnt is that we aren't responsible for other people's actions, we can only control our own reaction to any situation, and I had to let my guilt go. What is under our control is our decision to stay or leave, the way we react and whether we reach out for support. I had to learn to live life on my own to regain my strength, to find out who I was and what my purpose was, by reconnecting with myself and, by doing so, empowering myself to be the woman I am meant to be.

As a single mum now to three teenagers, working full time as a nurse, it was tough financially; the money stopped often before the end of the month, scratching for money to buy basic food supplies just to survive. It was hard. I am a proud person, not always wanting everyone to know my personal difficulties, as I feel everyone has their own issues to deal with. However, I knew that I had to reach out and bare my soul to say how bad we were financially. My children and I were now faced with other adversities. Hand on my heart, I can thank three human angels who came to my rescue at my time of need, we will be forever grateful to you, and your kindness to us all will never be forgotten. I have learnt that however tough life is and whatever obstacle is thrown in your way, that I am strong and resilient and to never give up.

The next turning point for me was when I saw a post on Facebook about a network marketing company opportunity in travel. I was instantly drawn to it as I love to travel. However, at first I was quite hesitant, wondering how it would work around my already busy life. My eyes were constantly being drawn back to it, so I reached out to the person who posted it and joined their team as a travel business owner and coach. This was a breath of fresh air for me, a new lease of life, having the flexibility to work my own hours around my day job. This gave me something for me to focus on to help have a better future for my children. It was exciting and opened up to me the possibilities of working towards my dream of a legacy and financial freedom. Within this industry, I found a community of like-minded people who came from different walks of life and different backgrounds. However, we all had one vision and came together as a team, supporting each other and lifting each other up when we were down. I joined this business just before national lockdown due to COVID-19, then lockdown happened. You may think, 'What a bad time to join a company?' No, it wasn't, as it gave me time to learn the ropes. I plugged into all the trainings and systems to learn about the industry and from the inspirational leaders within my team. If they could build a successful business, then so could I, with hard work, commitment and consistency, and for me to learn to trust the process as everything happens in its own time; I had to trust the timings of my life. I was on the way to creating a business of my dreams.

Within the network marketing industry, I have learnt the importance of having a strong mindset in business and in your personal life. I began to work on my own personal self-development and mindset. I joined the Femalepreneur Academy on personal recommendation from a friend; through their coaching and by using their tools and resources they have helped me to understand and reframe my thoughts, to refocus and to delve into the inner work, to unblock any negative and self-sabotaging thoughts. The day ahead might seem completely ordinary, but a mind shift could make it an extraordinary one. From feeling at rock bottom, I looked at myself in the mirror. Who did I see? Did I see me? This was eye-opening and a startling truth was staring right back at me. No, it wasn't me! In that moment, I knew I had to flip my mindset. The realisation that the only person to have control of my life was me, by flipping my mindset switch it allowed me to stop for a moment to realise that I can turn pain into power and to move forward to being resilient. By flipping my mindset switch, it allowed me to stop for a moment to realise that I can turn pain into power, to move forward to being resilient. Finding that inner strength to bounce back when I had every reason to shut down, but I continued to fight on, digging deep within myself and on my reserves, to enable me to overcome my setbacks and challenges. Everyone starts with their own baggage, their own negative and limiting beliefs and internal struggles. The only difference is the choices we make despite the challenges and obstacles in our way. Don't let your past define you or dictate your future. Being vulnerable is scary, but things that keep you stuck also set you free. It all starts with believing in yourself. Tapping into that inner strength and not letting the voice of fear dominate us. Never being afraid to dream big or to step outside of your comfort zone as that is when you grow and when the magic happens.

How has my life changed? Fast forward to the present – I'm excited about the future, I now surround myself with people who have warm energy, who light me up not drain me down, and people that lift me up. I totally believe your vibe attracts your tribe. Being authentic, being true and being you.

I was fortunate and incredibly lucky to be offered an opportunity recently with a global network marketing business in the beauty, health and wellness industry that was launching in the UK. This was an amazing opportunity, one that was offering me to become a founder in the company, and I felt this was a sign that was being put in front of me, one which I did not hesitate to join. I listened to my 'inner voice telling me to go for it' and I took that leap of faith, as I knew the leadership team was strong and that this could be something incredible. I continue to work full time and work my two network marketing businesses alongside this. My long-term vision is to sack my boss and work on my networking businesses full time, to gain time and financial freedom for myself and my children. Most of all, I enjoy seeing others within my team winning and I enjoy helping others fulfil their own dreams. Self-development and healing is a journey for me and I continue to work on my mindset every day, pushing down those negative, limiting beliefs that want to creep through. We are all human, we have good days and bad days, as long as we don't stay down for long and rise back up again.

Everyone has their own story to tell and, as I share my story, I want you to know that this has made me the strong, confident, resilient person I am today.

My message to you reading this: no matter what life throws at you, whatever the challenges, you don't have to face it alone, but it's up to you to take that step forward. Walk in your own truth. You are stronger than you think you are.

'You can rise up from anything,
You can completely recreate yourself,
Nothing is permanent,
You have choices,
You can think new thoughts,
You can learn something new,
You can create new habits,
All that matters is that you decide today and never look back.'

All my love to you all,
    Claire x

***

You can find Claire here:

https://mfacebook.com/public/
claire20%lowe?locate2=en_GB
https://m.facebook.com/discovertravel20/
https://facebook.com/happyhealthyyou21

# Trust the Process
## Candice Wilson

"What may seem like your worst nightmare may be
your best gift."

*I dedicate this chapter to all my amazing friends, old and new,
my family, my colleagues and my support team. Special thanks
to my sister who has always gone over and above the call of duty
to help me succeed.*

*My three wonderful daughters and four gorgeous grandchildren,
who gave me the strength to never give up and bring joy into my
each and every day.*

### Rejection

I was standing in the meeting room with my boss with
hope and optimism. My boss spoke, and I heard the
words, "You are not worthy."

That's not actually what my boss said; she said
nothing like that. However, it's what I heard at the time.

I felt I put a lot of energy into getting it right at work,

and now I was being told that I had to leave this job and go back to my previous post.

It may seem dramatic, but it felt like my world was falling apart. Things at home weren't great, my children had all flown the nest and my husband and I were outgrowing each other. My work was what kept me going and I put my heart and soul into it. The job rejection hit me to the core.

I knew deep inside that I should be doing something else with my life, that I had another calling, but fear held me back. I'd started a small business facilitating a group programme in the community that I had created and loved the results I was getting. However, I wasn't ready to leave the security of my job to pursue this as a career yet.

## Fear of Success

In a desperate bid to feel in control of my life and manage the horrific anxious feelings that came with fear, I made an appointment to see Marjorie. Marjorie had introduced me to an amazing technique called Silent Counselling and I needed to speak to her. She had reminded me many a time to trust the process but trying to trust was lost in amongst the fear, guilt, shame and pride. I shared my current situation with Marjorie… and what came up wasn't quite what I expected.

Fear of failure wasn't what was dominating me. It was in fact "fear of success". What unravelled during that

Silent Counselling session blew me away. I was in fact subconsciously frightened of my own power.

The next day, one week after that discussion with Marjorie, I handed in my notice. It was the best feeling in the world. I gained great kudos from my colleagues and it seemed I was eventually walking my talk.

Our eldest daughter was planning her wedding, we had a new baby grandson and I felt like my life was turning around.

DESPAIR

However, within the next few months, everything began to crumble rapidly.

My marriage was becoming very fragile, and the pressures of my self-employment wasn't helping. It was one thing being good at something, it was another thing running a business.

There was always so much to think about, and I found myself flitting from one thing to another, never getting anything finished. All the different roles in the business often left me feeling overwhelmed.

I also had a poor relationship with money, and despite the impact my coaching work was having, I struggled to ask for payment easily. I also struggled with budgeting. My confidence and capability may have been high, but my self-worth was on the floor.

Eventually my husband and I made a decision to part ways. I knew we were no longer aligned, and things weren't how we wanted them to be, but I was petrified of the impact this would have on my life. We'd been together since I was nineteen years old. I was now fifty and didn't have a clue about living independently.

As word started to trickle out, the shame was consuming me, with this "failure" programming going on in my mind. How could I run a business and inspire people? Who would listen to me when I couldn't get that most important relationship right?

HOPE

The day we shared with family and friends was tough and I had an appointment booked in with Marjorie. Again, she told me to trust the process and advised that she was very confident the Universe had big plans for me. I was so low that this concept didn't really work for me. How could I not have it all? A happy marriage and a great career isn't too much to ask, is it?

However, the very next day, something happened that blew me away.

I had been invited to a meeting where it looked like all my business dreams had come true. I was given what seemed an amazing opportunity and offered a lucrative position with an organisation who had a concept that I was super passionate about. I was to be a lead partner for this organisation in my country. The Universe was looking after me after all.

## LONELINESS

As much as there was lots of excitement around my business, I had by now moved into a rented property until I worked out where I wanted to be staying. It was a very lonely experience. Every day it felt like I was trying to manage this monster that was consistently in the pit of my stomach and at times felt unbearable.

I also missed so many parts of my old life. It maybe wasn't right, but it was very familiar to me. Angel readings became my new best friend as I became obsessed with trying to find out what path this was taking me on. I believed so much in the Universe yet couldn't allow myself to trust the process.

Most days I was out there inspiring and motivating people, whilst constantly needing reassurance from anyone who would tell me what I wanted to hear. This constant griping in my stomach kept me awake at night and I was so frustrated that I could not be the strong woman that I was known to be. I could cry at the drop of a hat.

## ADVENTURES

One restless night in November, I was still awake at 3am and felt compelled to watch *Eat, Pray, Love,* a film about a woman who went to Bali on a spiritual journey after her relationship with her husband started to crumble. As I watched the movie, my mind was racing – how could I do something life changing like this?

To cut a long story short, before I knew it, I was on my way to Thailand and joining fifteen other women on a volunteering trip, working in an elephant sanctuary then teaching English at a children's school in Cambodia.

This was truly a life-changing experience. I will be forever grateful for what that holiday taught me and chuckle often when I think of the day that I found my version of the medicine man at the Temples in Thailand. I was super excited to see him and asked the guides to take a photo of us together. He had this massive grin without any teeth and the guide couldn't stop laughing. He had asked her earlier to find him a wife and he had thought she had found him a very willing woman. Perception is a wonderful thing.

When I returned from the trip, I decided that the flat that I had moved into was no longer right for me. I moved in with my daughter and her partner for a while whilst looking for a new home. My family, friends and I searched for months to find somewhere that I would be happy to call home. Each time I went to view a property, my heart would sink deeper and deeper into despair. Yet again, that feeling of failure engulfed me. How had my life turned out like this when I had worked hard all my life? Four months after moving in with my daughter and her partner, I sat at the side of my bed and prayed. I wrote down everything I was looking for in a new home. It was very much a dream, but I asked for it, nevertheless.

Two weeks later, I found my dream place, with every single thing that I had asked for, including a sea view.

Finding my flat filled me with confidence that the

Universe really did have my back. Everyone who visits loves it and I am grateful every day for the gift of this home.

Before I knew it, I found myself in Holland on a five-day conference with the company that I was lead partner for. Here I was delivering a presentation for this organisation to colleagues from all over the world. At times I had to pinch myself at how my life was unfolding.

During this week, I connected strongly with one of the candidates called Henric, and over the next few years we became kindred spirits and went on to share an amazing business and friendship journey together. I often laugh at how I thought I had found "God" when I met Henric. He was extremely spiritual, and I embraced all the learnings I could during our times together.

## NEW LIFE UNFOLDING

I was living in my new flat and life was falling into place. I was meeting so many amazing people and having so many wonderful experiences. The beach was my haven, I went there when I needed answers now, I was really enjoying my life. Henric came to visit often, and I went to Norway, we ran retreats, seminars and workshops. We learned so much from each other and gained many new followers during this period.

## Wake Up in 2019 Seminar

Another great memorable experience was a seminar that I had a vision about in my dream one night. I managed to pull it together. Henric and my coach were key speakers, and many of my respected colleagues ran workshops for me and the clients. It was an amazing success with 100 candidates in attendance. My vision was to empower women to believe in themselves, something close to my heart as I had struggled with it myself for years.

## Business Coaching

Business ticked along over the next few years, but I knew that I was most definitely under-achieving.

I had a number of different coaches and joined various programmes; however, I never seemed to get the impact I expected or hoped for in my business. It always felt like something was missing but I didn't know what it was.

In fact, the coaching often left me feeling worse. All my coaches were telling me to put my prices up and reach out to people and I just couldn't seem to do it.

Every time it got to the money part, I would give discounts, added extras – never feeling I deserved to get paid my worth.

Covid-19 struck and I and many other business owners around the world went into panic. Clients cancelled and all my corporate work was postponed.

Again, my family were concerned for me and were sending me job opportunities, offering me to stay with them while everything was so fragile with my business.

In desperation, I signed up on a coaching programme that helped you get your business online. It seemed like the answer to my prayers. I had talked about running an online programme for years and never quite got round to doing it. I put my heart and soul into this training and gave it everything I had. However, again I would find I was comparing myself to others on the programme and would procrastinate when I could have been studying and could never work out what was wrong with me. Why did I keep on doing this?

On speaking to one of the coaches in the programme during the early days, he advised that I was self-sabotaging my business. I'm sure many people tried to tell me this over the years, but I never heard it.

This day, I very much heard it. It smacked me across the face like a lead balloon. Oh my goodness, I realised that I had actually been sabotaging most of my life. That's why everything slipped through my fingers, that's why I could never seem to "have it all". I didn't think I deserved to have it all.

Over the next few months, using energy healing and working with some amazing coaches, I managed to get to the root cause of why I was sabotaging and put to bed these limiting beliefs that came with low self-worth.

Once I became aware of the saboteur, I recognised that this too could be the problem for so many women in business. I started to see many with the same traits that I had: procrastinating, imposter syndrome, undercharging, overwhelm. Everything made so much sense. I desperately wanted to share this new-found knowledge with them.

I found the Femalepreneurs Academy and they become my new obsession, I drank in every mouthful of knowledge and expertise that they shared. Every time they spoke it was like they were speaking to me.

I had so much business knowledge now and realised that I could put a programme together and use my energy healing to help women out of self-sabotage and get to the root cause of what was holding them back.

I could offer a package that would include training in Silent Counselling and give them a skillset to use online, as well as helping them release all the energy blocks that were holding them back from their business.

I put my heart and soul into this programme, and this is how I spent most of lockdown. I had hope again and there was light at the end of the tunnel. I now had a small team incorporating a VA, copywriter and digital support supporting me, who were proving to be invaluable. Again, I was thinking about how this could help so many other women.

Best of You, Business Accelerator Programme was formed, and we are now halfway through the programme. It is filled with my dream clients and my business and my life are better than they have ever been, despite being in the midst of a pandemic. I have so much belief in myself and while many people have struggled during lockdown, I feel that the Universe has prepared me for this period in my life.

I look back now and can see why everything was happening for me and not to me. I had to go on this journey and learn what I had learned so that I could go on and help so many other women shine their light on a world that needs it more than ever now. I would never have believed that I would become an Ambassador and one of the few trainers who was sharing the magic of Silent Counselling with the world.

*Tribute to Sally, I promised you that when I became famous, I would remember you. I will forever be grateful for your completely unconditional friendship, love and understanding.*

★★★

You can find Candice here:

https://www.facebook.com/CandiceWilsonCoaching
www.candicewilson.co.uk
https://www.instagram.com/
candicewilsoncoaching/?igshid=x7m8fiocntgr

# IT IS NOT WHAT YOU DO, BUT WHO YOU ARE IN THE PROCESS

## Vicki Finnegan

*I dedicate this chapter to all the amazing women who have had that moment in their life of feeling lost, to those who have found the courage and strength to ask for help, and to those who feel scared to reach out. Please remember you can do this, you are amazing, reach within and you will find the strength.*

*To my amazing mother and my incredible friends and family who have supported me throughout this whole journey. I love you all so dearly, I am forever grateful to be so blessed to have you all in my life.*

*And finally, thank you to all the wonderful coaches and new friends whom I have been blessed to cross paths with. You have guided me on this journey and always believed in me, and for that I am eternally grateful.*

I am crumbling on the kitchen floor, staring out of the window, the tears rolling down my cheeks matching the raindrops dripping down the glass in the back door.

I have a heavy tight feeling in my chest, like someone is sitting on top of me, with a hand tightly wrapped around my heart squeezing the last bit of strength out of me.

I have always been the strong one, the one that holds everything together, the one that gets back up and carries on no matter the obstacle in my way. I was the one who had mastered putting anything that made me feel fear or not safe emotionally into a tightly squeezed box with a lid so tight no one could get in, just so I could get up each day and paint on a smile to face the world.

But not anymore. I could feel my heart shattering into tiny pieces. I was tired, I was exhausted.

I couldn't do it anymore. I had finally hit rock bottom; it just couldn't get any worse!

Rewind back a year, I was pregnant with my second baby boy and as much as I was bursting at the seams with excitement, I was also suffering with extreme morning sickness called Hyperemesis Gravidarum, making day to day life extremely difficult. I couldn't work, I couldn't drive, I couldn't eat, I couldn't drink, I couldn't even pick my first-born up from nursery. I was almost bed bound and it was having a huge effect on me and my family, as you can imagine.

At twenty-seven weeks pregnant, I was starting to feel a bit more normal, or as normal as you can be in your third trimester. We had started preparing for a house move, packing up our rented property. We were buying our first home and had been waiting for this moment for what felt like forever, something we had been dreaming of and finally it was happening, we could be a family of four in our first home.

Just as things were coming together, a family trauma hit and broke us all into a thousand pieces. I was heavily pregnant, only weeks away from giving birth. We were living between two houses and I was watching my loved ones crumble around me.

I had to be strong, I had to be strong for my family, I had to be strong for my partner and I had to be strong for my children.

Somehow, we managed to keep going, we were getting through each day, each week, each month, but what choice do you have, you just have to keep going, don't you?

I was carrying on with a painted-on smile, not just for me, but for everyone else too; for my newborn baby, unbeknown to him what kind of tragedy he had just arrived in. For my eldest son, whose world had just been turned upside down and who had now been given the role of big brother, he was no longer the only child. For my partner who was going through pain, like I had never witnessed in my life, and for my family who were all trying to piece back some sort of normality that just did not feel right for anyone.

The new year came, we had been in our new house adjusting to being a family of four for the past four months, still grieving and coming to terms with how life had changed for us all and, whilst everyone else was full of elation for a new year and a new start, I was full of dread. My maternity leave was coming to an end and

I was filled with anxiety about heading back to work. I was still breastfeeding my little one, and although to others this may not seem to be a big deal, for me this was causing me anxiety and becoming a huge obstacle. My little one refused a dummy; I had literally tried every single kind going to help him with teething but no joy. He also refused to take a bottle, which didn't make much difference as I had struggled to express throughout my breastfeeding journey, so feeding was limited to just me. I was faced with the predicament of how I would get around the bedtime routine and keeping my little one fed whilst at work.

On top of this, I was going back to a job I had fallen out of love with. I was living on autopilot, events from the past playing on my mind, weighing me down and living a mediocre life that I was desperate to change but just did not know how to.

My eldest son's behaviour was rapidly deteriorating, and I felt like I was a failure with being a mum, a partner, and just failing at life in general. I longed for a way out, I longed for something or someone to help us as a family and I longed to remember what it felt like to smile with feeling, with passion and true happiness. I just didn't know how or where to find it.

So here I was, breaking down on my kitchen floor, feeling lonely and scared. I was scared to reach out, scared to admit I wasn't coping and just full of anxiety. I couldn't keep it in anymore; surely there had to be more to life than this? I deserved to be happy again, didn't I? My family deserved to smile again!

Little did I know this was the point of my breakthrough, this was the first time I had prayed and asked for help. I'm not religious nor do I have anything against religion, but I felt a need to reach out and ask for help. I lifted my head and for the first time of what now has become many, I saw a little black bird, sitting on a branch right outside the door, looking straight at me. And in that moment, I just knew, I knew things were going to change, I had been listened to, I had been heard. I didn't know how, and I didn't know when, but life was about to change.

Next came the start of many miracles. I had manifested not one but two new business adventures that were completely out of my comfort zone and which I knew nothing about, but it gave me that fire in my belly, filled me with passion and an exhilarating feeling I had missed for so long. It was the missing piece in my life. I had felt so unfulfilled for so long even though I had a good job and had worked hard over the years to build my career to a good level in management with a particularly good salary, but I still felt lost, I felt like I was missing something.

I remember saying to my partner I know this seems crazy, but I just know this business adventure is going to change our lives, it is going to give us everything we could ever wish for. As I said these words out loud, I had this overwhelming feeling that I can only explain as tingles, which filled my entire body from head to toe. It felt like a fountain of emotions spilling out of me, so much joy, happiness, excitement that made me cry happy tears. Anyone looking in would think I was crackers, but I just knew this was the start of something incredible.

Unbeknown to me I manifested my redundancy, and when the news came, I was smiling from ear to ear. I can hear you saying now, is she crazy? But this redundancy was a blessing in disguise. The decision had been made for me and I was able to work from home, around my family and put my all into my new businesses. I wasn't worried, I wasn't scared, I felt no fear, I just knew this was all meant to happen; it was all happening for me not to me.

My black bird continued to visit me at those moments I needed reassurance or had a decision to make, and people started to come into my life who helped me to believe in who I am, guided me to find my life purpose and helped me to become who I am today.

Things started changing and I was starting to see a new path unfolding whilst making new friendships with people who I know will be in my life for many years to come.

I was guided to begin what I now know was the start of my spiritual awakening, my healing journey, which has completely changed my perspective on life and led me on to release that trapped little girl deep inside who had been suffering for years, screaming to get out and be heard. The girl who had been made to feel worthless, had no confidence, like she didn't belong. The girl who wasn't good enough, cool enough and didn't fit in, when all she ever wanted was to feel like she belonged.

After peeling back the layers one by one, I've

removed years of limiting beliefs, negative emotions and conditioning we have all grown accustomed to. I have forgiven those from my past, who have caused me pain, suffering and hurt, going right back to being a little girl, when I was bullied from a young age and through my school years. I have let go of events and moments in my life that I had no idea had caused me to feel stuck and stopped me from being me. Whilst discovering that these moments in my life have led me to make certain decisions and affected my behaviour over and over again throughout the years.

However, what I will say is, I don't regret one thing or the way my life has panned out, because these have been my learnings that have made me into the woman I am today.

These are the learnings that have made me stronger, helped me remove fear and doubt, and helped me believe in myself; believe I am worthy; believe I am enough.

Sometimes life can throw you curveballs that can make you feel like your world is falling apart, and, in those moments, it really is so hard to believe you can get through it. You can't even begin to think how everything will work out for you or how you are going to get through each day; where do you go next, what steps do you need to take and who can you actually turn to? Thankfully, I had my mum by my side. I don't know what I would have done without her if I didn't reach out that day when I needed her the most. She has been my rock, and I am eternally grateful to have such a beautiful kind soul as my mother.

If you ever feel like this, I ask you, please don't be afraid to ask for help and I don't just mean turning to a person, a friend or a loved one. I mean saying those words out loud, 'I'm asking for help, show me, guide me, help me.'

You don't have to be religious, and you don't have to have an answer to who you're talking to. It could be God, a spirit, an angel, a loved one passed or the universe. It is completely up to you and what you feel comfortable with. What you come to believe will unfold in time if you are willing to watch the magic unfold.

The key is to look out for little signs; it could be a bird reappearing, feathers along your path, songs you're suddenly drawn to with a hidden message or the people who come into your life at that time. You may not be able to understand what is happening, but you will get to a point in your life where you can look back and think, ahh that will be why that happened then, and you will be able to begin to piece it all together.

Just don't ever give up, trust the journey and when those moments are hard, don't take it as a personal attack. See it as a moment of learning, what can you learn from it? How can this make you stronger, wiser, more fulfilled? How can it lead you onto becoming the best version of you?

I have learnt so much about myself on this journey so far and I am only just beginning, because we are always evolving, we will always have a new layer to peel. I have learnt that energy is everything, I have learnt that the universe has always got my back and I have learnt that I can have, do or be anything I want. We all have the power within us to live the life we desire as long as we believe in ourselves.

Don't ever be afraid to invest in yourself, always believe you are worthy and deserve the investment. What can feel so scary in that moment could actually change your life and be the missing link you have been yearning for. The best thing I ever did was invest in the Femalepreneur Academy, not only has this been a huge part of my journey of self-discovery and healing, but it has also been a huge part in finding who I am as a business owner. I have gained so much personally whilst building an incredible friendship with two amazing women, full of wisdom and knowledge, who guide you through everything. Natasha and JoJo, I can't thank you both enough for everything you have done for me, I am forever grateful. As much as this journey has been hard, it has been completely worth it, and I have enjoyed every moment.

When you feel like things are falling apart, just know it's all coming together for you behind the scenes. Trust that the universe is helping everything work out in your favour for you. And In your darkest of moments, when you feel like giving up on life, remember they are actually your turning points.

Your new lease of life is waiting for you, your higher self is waiting to connect with you, and your spirit guides are always there to help you. And, most importantly, always remember it's not what you do, it's who you are in the process.

\*\*\*

You can find Vicki here:

Linktree:
https://linktr.ee/vickiTiana

Website:
http://travelwithvicki.com

# Not Letting Others Define You by Your Disability – My truth

## Victoria Woodbridge

*In loving memory of my beautiful grandmother Rowena for teaching me to always speak my truth, my brother for setting me on my mission in life, my children Reuben, Scarlett-Rose and Harper and my partner Dean for always being patient with me on this journey and my bumpy days, for changing his life and becoming the full-time carer, for our first-born daughter. I am grateful to him for always supporting me to embrace my passions and always having faith in me no matter how tough times can be for us as a family… I love you all! Oh, and especially to my father, for always instilling in me that failure is not an option!!*

Do you ever think in life we are here for a specific purpose, that our life purpose has already been set for us, that there is no such thing as chance, and everything happens for a reason that guides us directly onto our destined path?

Most people expect life to be a certain way but to me it's more like a sailboat. You intend to go in one certain

THE ELEVATION OF THE *Femalepreneur*

direction, but the wind can take you in a completely different direction. There are rocky seas and I truly have had my share; I still have many and I am sure so many more are in my life to come! However, if I have learnt anything so far in my life, it's to ride each storm that passes and to ride each one with pride.

There are rocky seas, which are then followed by calm seas. The sea is like a comparison of life itself in turn, which like life has its ups and its downs, and we go through certain stages. But it is all about adjusting our sails to the direction of the wind or our life's path. You have to survive the storms and endure the struggles if you want to see the good and what life is truly about and those moments that make it all completely worth it!

I have had to learn more in later years of my life that things will not go to plan the majority of the time, especially if you are faced with adversity or your path is naturally a bit more of a bumpy ride than others. Sometimes life is challenging and sometimes it's just goddamn hard! But never have any regrets and learn from each challenge or situation you are given, or the cards you have been dealt.

Sometimes it is those great big crashing waves and the darkest of storms, it's these moments that test us the most and guide our sails or set our life's path in a different direction… A better direction. For me, I have learnt that sometimes GROWTH can only occur in the deepest and most painful of situations that we encounter. Sometimes in those situations we find our true and real meaning of our lives, if we are just brave enough to listen… and it is then, if we truly listen, we might just hear the why and our true purpose.

Just because there are storms and dark nights doesn't mean life isn't beautiful… to me this is WHY life is so beautiful, to look through the dark nights and the storms and still see the beauty. It's in those challenges and in that contrast that I have truly discovered my life's greatest gifts and true purpose.

Ever since I was a young girl, I was born an empath and into a caring role, having an older sibling registered blind. I have known from a very young age what it was like for a sibling to struggle daily, I watched the frustration, the sadness, the loneliness, the isolation and the feeling of no one understanding. I knew and I learnt about people's total lack of care and complete ignorance towards others with differences and disabilities. I learnt the fact that if it wasn't a part of their 'bubble' or 'world' and it wasn't affecting them, then it wasn't relevant, and it really didn't matter.

In fact, I learnt the true meaning of actual blindness, which was not so much my brother's condition but more of the people and the world around us and their complete blindness and total ignorance, which on the contrary caused much more of an issue for my brother and us as a family than my brother's condition itself. I learnt how cruel the world and the people in it can be, the awful things people can say and do, the shame, ridicule and humiliation others can cause a person and the damage this causes, just for being a little different to them. Which I am sure so many other people and families have encountered themselves.

I learnt especially the use of the disgusting and offensive words such as 'mentally retarded' and 'spastic', which were used to describe my brother often just for having a vision impairment. Which, in fact again, was so far from the truth for my brother, who is one of the most intelligent people I have ever had the privilege of knowing. Although he does not know this, growing up, at times I was in complete and total envy of him; he was so much more advanced in things compared to me, actually in several things really (but I never would tell him that). He could just do things I could in no way do, but only long and wish I could do. Like his ability to remember masses and masses of information from memory and how he could recite things and information from the top of his head like he was reading it out of a textbook, but it was all purely from memory. He was and still is far from those disgusting and offensive words that were used to describe people for having a vision loss, some of which are still being used today.

The treatment my brother received, and we encountered as a family, made me quite angry and wanting to change the views and the perception of those around me, but on a far greater scale. Whether their views were through pure ignorance, being frightened to be associated with someone who was a little different or whether it was just not understanding and the lack of awareness and education on these things, I knew that I would be teaching people these things one day.

My older brother was born with two conditions known as Retinitis Pigmentosa and Congenital

Nystagmus, which are two different types of vision loss. Roughly around two million people worldwide suffer from Retinitis pigmentosa, which is a rare eyesight disorder, causing a gradual eyesight loss and can lead to total blindness. The other condition Congenital Nystagmus causes uncontrolled eye movement, in which the eyes will move or "wobble" constantly. My brother was born with these conditions at birth and both conditions are not treatable with no cure, and are lifelong conditions.

Due to my upbringing and being a very protective younger sibling, I always knew, and I just had this overwhelming sense of purpose, that no matter what I would do with my life I would always be advocating for individuals and raising disability awareness. I would ultimately embrace and embark on this journey throughout my adulthood. This would be to challenge stigma and support those with disabilities, including 'hidden disabilities', allowing them to feel comfortable to share with others that they have a disability and not to worry about being judged, harassed or ridiculed and to raise awareness of the unacceptable terminology still being used when describing individuals that may not be the so-called 'normal' to others.

Evidence shows that some of the most iconic, successful and creative geniuses that have ever lived on this planet are actually those associated with being the oddest and most bizarre people on this planet. Such as Leonardo Da Vinci, Mozart, Beethoven and Michelangelo, which is to name just a few. But just think where we would actually be today without what some of these extraordinary individuals accomplished in their lifetime.

With this burning desire since a child to help others, I decided that when I left school at seventeen, after completing my A levels, I was going to go straight into work. This is when I started voluntary work for the Royal Association for the Deaf (RNID), then working my way up into the management team, achieving my level five management diploma in health and social care. I worked for RNID for around eleven years, learning the beauty of sign language and Braille. Learning how to support those who were deaf and also deafblind individuals with disabilities ranging from mental health, stroke, multiple sclerosis, epilepsy, diabetes, dementia, autism, learning disabilities and other health conditions.

After I left RNID, I was an area manager of another care provision and then became an NVQ health and social care assessor. It was not until I had my second child that my world was completely turned upside down and I was faced with a completely different reality and a world totally unknown to me. Now it was my turn...

My first daughter Scarlett Rose was born with extreme complications; upon delivery, she suffered from lack of oxygen, aspirated her meconium and was having severe seizures. I saw her for a few seconds before she was rushed down to the special care baby unit where she was intubated, put on life support and into cooling, to try and prevent further seizures and brain damage occurring and to support her breathing as she was having difficulty breathing by herself.

This was one of the most life altering and changing moments of my life, not only as a parent and being frightened we would lose our baby and being told the next seventy-two hours were vital for our baby in whether she would survive, but this also triggered a high amount of trauma for me that has now caused lifelong disabilities and changes to my health both physically and mentally. At the time I did not realise this had occurred to me until the months to follow.

Scarlett, being the strong and determined little one she is, pulled through after spending six weeks in the special care baby unit. When we left hospital, it was still unknown to us at this point what physical and other health complications Scarlett might face in the future and what life would be like for her as she got older. We left the hospital and at that time Scarlett was NG fed by a syringe as she was unable to feed like other babies, which was really heartbreaking, as I just wanted to breastfeed. But this was unsuccessful and so was bottle feeding. So, we NG fed Scarlett every three hours for the first six months of her life.

Within my life I have always played the caring role, but never would I have expected to do this for one of my children, as a parent, for a child with high complex medical needs. Scarlett now is three, she is now PEG fed, she has general developmental delay, suffers from epilepsy, reflux, eyesight problems, with 50% less vision in one eye, high astigmatisms and a squint, mobility issues, including low muscle tone and weakness. She needs a wheelchair when her mobility is poor at home and when going out if she gets really tired, to try and prevent falls, as she regularly falls over and injures herself. She still has swallowing difficulties, a speech difficulty and delay and a nut allergy. We are still waiting for further tests on a possible diagnosis of Cerebral palsy, as we still have not been given an official diagnosis as to why Scarlett was born with these complications leading to needing PEG feeding and intervention and having all the other health problems she has. We are constantly in and out of hospital and she is under twelve medical professionals.

However, through these tough times, I have seen pure beauty. Scarlett is a total inspiration and never have I met someone with so much strength. She never complains, she is never down, never does she stop smiling, she is one of the happiest little ones you will ever meet and never lets any of her challenges get in her way. Scarlett just loves living and loves life (as everyone who knows her will also say). I know Scarlett will always do well no matter what she faces in the future as she has already learnt from such a young age the core principles and values it takes to succeed in life; strength, determination, confidence. She definitely knows what she wants at all times and she lets nothing get in her way. I am truly one proud mumma!

Things became very different for me after I had Scarlett. Not only did I have a disabled baby, I then suffered with my own mental health issues from the trauma and what we went through, which caused me to suffer from severe anxiety and depression. In the early days after having Scarlett, I couldn't even leave the house and then I found out as well I had fibromyalgia. So, I was faced with a disabled baby and a very different version of me. I was the carer but now my world had flipped, and I was the one facing health challenges and difficulties myself and looking at the world from a very different viewpoint.

I found it very hard to come to terms with the changes and the effects it had on my life, from struggling to get out of bed, the constant pain and fatigue, the changes it had on my relationship, and this very different and new person I had become. But I was determined and still am to not allow this to ever limit me or hold me back, but instead I used this to redefine myself and it gave me a new sense of purpose and the strength to rewrite my own story on my terms and set myself a new journey; what could be more amazing than that? In a sense, I felt reborn.

It was strange that I was now the one experiencing how my brother must have felt at times and some of the people I have supported. I now have a very different personal viewpoint of knowing what having a disability feels and looks like, as I am seeing it first-hand and living with it daily.

But it was always through these extremely difficult times and moments in my life that I have learnt the most and it has brought me onto my path to the wonderful things I am now achieving, which I never thought would have even been possible before. I have now learnt my disability is a part of my diversity, so this is very much my identity and I won't be ashamed or embarrassed of the new person I have become. I make the most of each day I have with my children and my partner and try to achieve the best I can, not only for me, but for them as well.

I am now halfway through my university degree in qualifying to be a speech and language therapist, I continue to support the deaf community and HOH individuals, as this is something I will always be passionate about. I am working closely with a company called Bounce, which is a life insurance brokerage to help deaf and HOH individuals have better access when it comes to life and funeral insurance by providing all inclusivity within the insurance sector. In the very near future, I will be training to be the first UK life insurance advisor that is able to sign for deaf clients.

I am completing level six British sign language and soon will be a qualified and accredited deaf awareness trainer and I have just launched a sign language clothing and merchandise brand, to support British sign language and raise awareness for this beautiful language. It was also through starting university that I learnt that I had dyslexia and dyspraxia, both undiagnosed since I was a child.

So, having these tough moments, it is these very moments that have been the true making of me and have given me my life purpose. The purpose that had already been created and instilled in me since I was a child and now with my disabilities and challenges, I feel like I have come full circle for my life purpose. I can speak my own truth on how it feels and make an even bigger difference.

Sometimes life throws you a curveball. I caught mine and went with the curve and no matter what life brings for me or my family, I will always continue to show my children that we can achieve and will achieve, our differences make us unique and are in essence the making of us! We still write our own stories; nothing is impossible, and everything is possible.

I count my blessings each day I wake up, even on the bumpy days; I have learnt to ride each storm with my own energy and unique spirit!

I end on this part for my brother where my true mission and life purpose first began, as he loves to say 'to dare is to do'.

★★★

You can find Victoria here:

https://www.facebook.com/Deafinsure01
https://www.facebook.com/groups/httpswww.
lifeanddeaf.info
https://www.linkedin.com/in/victoria-
woodbridge-538133167/
www.deafinsurancegroup.co.uk

# You Are Stronger Than You Think

## Emma Nottage

*I dedicate my chapter to my loving family who have supported
me throughout my life, including my amazing parents
who are 'the wind beneath my wings' and my wonderful
husband Stuart, who is my rock and partner in life's glorious
adventure. I also dedicate this chapter to the many teachers who
championed me through my educational years and helped to
shape me into the person who I am today. Finally, I dedicate
this chapter to all those women who like me have faced obstacles
in life's rich tapestry and I want to encourage you all that it is
never too late… until it is too late. So, seize the moment now
and step out onto the water that is prepared for you.*

Do you follow your dreams? The words of others over us
can be a powerful thing. So many of us in life have been
bruised and damaged by the words that someone has
spoken over us. As a music teacher I have come across so
many adults who tell me sad tales of being told in their
childhood that they 'were not good enough to sing in the
school choir' or that they 'were not good enough to play
in the band' or that their parents wouldn't let them learn

the instrument of their choice, which took away their enjoyment and love of music.

I can relate to their stories as, although music has always surrounded me and been a part of my life, there was one event that might have stopped me in my tracks. In infant school I started playing the recorder and also the piano but when I got to junior school, I wanted to learn to play the guitar. I had an audition to do so and was denied the opportunity of reaching that dream at that point because the guitar teacher made a snap decision there and then that I could not hold the instrument correctly and was not able to do it. I don't remember clearly exactly how these words made me feel but I am sure that they must have affected me at the time, as I still remember the event now. I didn't let it stop me, though, and I went on to excel in the French horn (considered the most difficult instrument) and had my voice trained. I went on to study music at A Level and then gained a BA degree in Music. I then followed that with a Post Graduate Certificate in Education with specialism in seven-to-eleven years and music teaching. During my teacher training year, I taught myself how to play the guitar and it has now come full circle, as guitar is one of the many instruments that I teach to adults and children. If I had let the words and actions of that guitar teacher from my primary school years stop me in my tracks, then I would not be writing this to you today as the successful global music teacher that I am and I want to say to you that you can do the same – follow your musical dreams or any big dream you might have. It lights me up when I help adult music students to find and develop their voice or to play a musical instrument that they have always wanted to.

My word of the year for 2021 is 'resilience' and this is something that has been necessary to develop over the course of my life. In my childhood and early teenage years, I was very shy and did experience some bullying at school. It was through music, dance and drama that my confidence greatly developed, and I found 'my tribe'. I found the ability to stand up on stages taking part in performing arts festivals, dance shows and music concerts. I have always had 'stickability' and the only activity I gave up in childhood was gymnastics because one of the instructors was quite strict and wanted me to perform the gymnastic move 'the forward roll' before I felt I was ready to, so in the end I left the club. I loved the performing arts and they also enabled me to develop a thicker skin as you are graded and judged in front of many others through them. I danced three times a week between the ages of five to eighteen. I knew I wasn't the best dancer at my dance school, I found it hard to remember all the steps in our dances from week to week and some of the younger girls progressed far quicker than I did, but this was never an issue between us as we were like one big family. Looking back now, though, I think that subconsciously it did affect me, and I wished that I could be as good and as far forward as some of my younger friends there were. I also did speech and drama through my dance school and it was when I did a 'Song and Dance' routine that my friend's mum said to my mum, 'She's got a really good voice, you should get it trained,' that my journey into singing also took off. At first my piano teacher taught me to sing but then she said that my talent was beyond her, so she passed me onto a wonderful singing teacher friend of hers. He was amazing and really developed my vocal ability along with my confidence. Sadly, though, after a few years, I lost him as unknown to me he was awaiting a triple heart bypass surgery and unfortunately it came too late, and he actually passed away doing something he loved – adjudicating singing in a festival. I went on to have two further great singing teachers in college and university who further developed my voice. I also have a lot to thank my main French horn teacher for too, as he was also an instrumental supporter and role model in my teenage years.

I also owe so much to certain academic teachers throughout my school years who really believed in me and encouraged me to forge my path. In the infant school, my learning was a bit behind, but in junior school and privately I received extra literacy and maths help. This definitely paid off as by the time I was eleven years old I had a reading age of a fourteen-year-old and also knew all my multiplication tables. If I had not had resilience and worked hard with these teachers, then I would not be writing this for you here today. Also, in my childhood, I had physical health issues that I had to work through. I am an asthmatic and often had to sit out of PE lessons at school. I also had to see a private ear, nose and throat specialist as I had ear problems during my childhood and my left eardrum perforated a total of five times. If it had perforated one more time before I was fourteen, I would have had to have had surgery to replace it but thankfully it did not and now my hearing is very good, and I always received top marks in the aural part of my music examinations. I have needed resilience in my musical journey too. For example, in my teenage years I had to wear a 'train track' brace on my top teeth and was told that I might have to stop playing my horn for a while. Instead, I was determined to continue to not fall behind, so I kept on playing and built stamina and resistance by putting up with the pain of my mouthpiece pressing on my lips and the inside of my mouth being ripped by my brace. But I did it. During this time, I also took my grade five horn exam and unfortunately failed it, but again, I didn't let that stop me and I re-took the exam, this time passing with distinction. I went on to gain my grade six and grade eight horn exams and I also gained my grade eight certificates in voice and in music theory.

Resilience has also been a necessary quality in my personal and emotional life too. In my adult life I finally faced and conquered through Cognitive Behavioural Therapy my Tokophobia (fear of pregnancy and childbirth) that had been with me since my teenage years. The journey has not continued to be easy though, as since conquering that debilitating fear, my husband and I were not able to conceive a child easily and were placed into the '10% unexplained infertility' category. We both underwent several tests and the only thing that they found was that I had a very slightly underactive thyroid level. So, I started taking Levothyroxine and, shortly after this, four years ago I did finally conceive for the first time. Once again, though, our story was not one of plain sailing as sadly we lost that pregnancy and my right fallopian tube when I had to undergo emergency surgery for an advanced and complex ectopic pregnancy. I had not really known anything of the condition before but now I know that one in eighty pregnancies turns out to be ectopic and there is no way of saving an ectopic pregnancy. I am also very thankful to be here to write this to you today as I was told by my surgeon the morning after my surgery, 'We saved your life.' My Christian faith helped me through this traumatic experience, and I have a story of witness from this time. When I was left in a hospital room with my mum waiting to be taken to the ward before my surgery, my mobile phone suddenly beeped at 12pm and I looked down and saw that I had a text message. At the start of the month I had signed up to something called 'Ten Days of Grace' that I had seen advertised by a Christian radio station on Facebook. It was for a different encouraging Bible verse to come through to your phone at 12pm for ten days. I had forgotten about it in all the roller coaster of that week and when I looked at the message at that moment I was overcome with emotion as it said: "Peace I leave with you; my peace I give you. I do not give to you as the world gives. Do not let your hearts be troubled and do not be afraid." (John 14 verse 27). I felt my heart in my mouth and a sense of calm and peace wash over me. I looked at my mum and I said, 'It's okay. He's (Jesus) got me.' And I just knew that whatever happened I was going to be all right. Sadly, my pregnancy was not viable, and we lost that dream of becoming parents that time, but there is still hope for the future. We are still trying to naturally conceive but we may also go down the road of adoption in the future. The experience has made me much more pragmatic, and I often now say, 'It is what it is.' I faced all my fears at once and found an inner strength that I never knew I had. My husband and I have found that by being honest and open with people about our struggles along our journey, it has enabled others to approach us and share their vulnerabilities with us, and we feel that we have been able to help so many people. Our Christian faith has strengthened and encouraged us both in these difficult times, as we know that we are not alone and that our faithful and loving God is upholding us. I truly believe that I was put on this earth to be an encourager and that is what I aim to do every day. I hope that you are encouraged reading this chapter.

In my career I have been a primary school teacher for twenty-two years and a private one-to-one music tutor alongside this for seventeen years. During the current global pandemic, as an asthmatic, I decided to step out of the classroom and back from my face-to-face lessons. At the start of the first lockdown, I felt quite low but then my resilience arose again, and I kicked myself into action and transitioned to online music teaching. I set myself up a website for my business after years of never having one and I created business pages for my music teaching on

Facebook and Instagram. I also started attending online networking meetings and have now totally embraced the online space and the opportunities that it has provided for me. I have retained most of my local students and I now also have students across the UK and even some students in the USA and other parts of the globe. I am also becoming known as a 'go to' expert online in the field of music education and how music relates to and enhances our life, learning and health. I created my musical discussion group on Facebook eight months ago and it now has over two hundred interactive members. I have done a weekly LIVE show on a different musical topic each week and we are working towards doing a seven-day musical challenge together in the group. I love serving my group members and sharing my passion for music and its rightful place in education and society. I am also in the process of writing my first non-fiction book all about music and how it relates to and enhances our spiritual, physical, emotional and mental health. I am creating an online course/programme about how we can use music to improve our mental health as I feel that this is so needed in our world at this time. I hope to launch a podcast around these same subjects in the future.

I want to end by drawing your imagination to a picture painted for me by my talented friend who is a Christian artist. She painted it after I asked if she could represent a vision that I had experienced. The painting is a fictional one of me standing in the end of a rowing boat on a beautiful lake surrounded by mountains. In front of me, walking on the surface of the water is the figure of Jesus dressed all in white, opening his arms out to me. At the bottom of the painting is written a simple phrase: 'Step out of the boat'. This was a message to me in my fertility journey, but I believe that it can also be a lesson for all of us in our lives. We don't need to be afraid to be brave and take that first step out of our comfort zone. We are stronger than we think, and we are never alone. So, my challenge to you is: What are you waiting for? Follow your dreams and… Step out of the boat.

★★★

You can find Emma here:

www.musicaldiamond.com
emma@musicaldiamond.com
https://www.facebook.com/Mrs-Emma-Nottage-Private-Music-Tutor-103166971432105
www.instagram.com/emmanottagemusictutor

# MILKSHAKES & DREAMS
## Laura Griffiths

*I'm dedicating this chapter to everyone who was born with a feeling in their soul never to settle for average and every person throughout my journey so far who has shown me how to do things, and importantly how not to do things.*

*This is for my son Marcus, who shows me every day there is a different way to think about things.*

*This is also for my family, especially Mum, whose strength has carried all of us through the dark times.*

I'm going to describe a feeling that I've never been able to put into words or even tried to explain to another person but it is a feeling that I had throughout my childhood and most of my adult life that is like a physical homesickness, even though I got this especially when I was at home. I would get this over and over again but could never put my finger on what was causing me to feel like it. I would go through every logical possibility in my mind and then tell myself I had no reason to feel like this. It would appear and disappear out of nowhere but I could never completely shake this strange feeling off. I did know it was linked to a feeling that I wasn't here for ordinary and I just had an inner belief I was here for something bigger but the problem I had was never knowing what the 'big' thing was, so most of my career I struggled with a silent battle that I should know clearly what I was supposed to be doing and the role I was supposed to play in life, but I didn't. Looking back, I can now see I wasn't supposed to be defined by this thing but actually I just needed to be in control of my own destiny because you can be a mixture of all the things you want. I felt like I was waiting for something but, because I didn't have a clear dream of what it was, I only found it by learning what it was not.

At school I did enough to play the game to get to where I thought I needed to be. I went to university and I naively had huge dreams for the difference I wanted to make in the world. I would be working for the UN and doing something on a global scale, I wasn't destined for an ordinary job because I wanted a life that really made a difference and not just in a small way.

My first job upon finishing university wasn't as a United Nations peacekeeper after all but instead I stumbled into a role working for a multi-millionaire who had huge faith in me and gave me opportunities that anywhere else I would have had to work an entire career to gain. Despite this, it still did not leave me satisfied, but showed me a glimpse of a life I wanted... not to be part of someone else's dream but I needed to create my own. I think from this point in my very first job I knew I would not settle until I had created the life and lifestyle I wanted on my own terms.

Without knowing how to achieve this vague dream, I followed a career and went for jobs that I thought were always better than the last job I had, but I was always led back to working with entrepreneurs, business owners, business start-ups, business support organisations and people who also had big dreams. I discovered quickly in my career that I struggled to work for corporate companies and early on in one company I got told I was 'unmanageable as an employee'. I was always secretly rather proud of this statement, but the problem really was I didn't like to be told what to do. However, I also recognised I had a huge respect and admiration for people who were running their own empires. I hated having the restrictions placed on my life that I felt a job gave you and being accountable to other people who to me were just stopping me achieving my own dreams. Even writing this my heart sinks thinking about being controlled by what days and times you can work, when you can go away and how long for, pay scales, appraisals, career ladders, not choosing who you deal with and even whether you can walk out for a coffee when you feel like it, these are all things I feel are my basic rights and I should determine for myself! I'm unsure where the idea came from (maybe because it was a global event and the biggest sporting event in the world on my search for great purpose) but I always knew I wanted to in some way be part of the 2012 Olympics when they came to

London, so I decided the best way to achieve this would be to volunteer. The company I worked for at the time wouldn't allow me to take the leave. Although I know nobody likes to be told no, deep down I really had trouble accepting this and it wasn't because I wouldn't be able to take part in my Olympic dream, but because it confirmed: *I was not in charge of my destiny*.

Still not knowing what I was really looking for but still searching for this 'great' thing, I wanted something on a grander and bigger scale, so I wanted to move to and work in London; maybe that would leave me satisfied and people would see my true potential. As I didn't want to work in just any place, I accepted a job in Canary Wharf and was based in what at the time was one of the tallest buildings in the UK. Here, surely, I would find people like me all following their dreams and I would be where I needed to be? I did not find this, it was quite the opposite… prestigious offices but not prestigious goings on, and people that did not even know what they were doing it all for. However, amongst this I yet again came across another entrepreneur who had had the most amazing career, owned multiple businesses, travelled the world and was friends with some of the world's most famous people, but above all they had such a presence, kindness and dignity, which was everything I admired. Being at another turning point in the job I was doing, he asked me if I wanted to work for him. I do believe it was worth the terrible previous job just to get that opportunity, but this person had rented an office I was managing and had just happened to win one of the main contracts, which was a major part of the organising of the London 2012 Olympics! I had done it without even trying, I had found a way to be part of the Olympics. I didn't say it out loud but smiled at the thought that I had been refused to take unpaid leave for it but now I would be at the centre of it and even be paid for it. Finally, I had a role that I felt I was supposed to have, with this huge event that I had really wanted to be part of and was working right alongside the person in charge of it. For the first time it really did give me a feeling that I was where I should be, but then what happened? It was a contract, the London Olympics would end and, of course, so would my role too.

So, what next? How would any another employment compare? I think I knew nothing would, as that was such a unique experience that couldn't ever happen again. Any job after that I felt would be a huge disappointment. Although it was not a deliberate choice I can see, after this I had decided subconsciously that the greatest thing I could do next was to become a mum, looking after a whole new life, what could be more important than that? Maybe that is what I was here for, maybe that search for what I was here to do I could fulfil with motherhood. Becoming a mum did not come easy to me and, although I love my son very much, I knew deep down that my main purpose wasn't just to be a mum; rightly or wrongly, I wasn't comfortable just being a mum, it wasn't how I saw myself.

When my son was nearly one year old, once again I was left thinking, 'What am I here to do? How am I going to satisfy that feeling that I have achieved what I'm really here for?' I scanned for jobs half-heartedly that I had no interest in and I did not really even want. I hoped I wouldn't find anything suitable because everything felt like such a step backwards and there was no doubt it would be much harder now with my extra responsibilities.

I wanted to create something better, so I decided that was the last time I would work for anyone else; I just knew I wouldn't be happy. I began to see there was a reason all these entrepreneurs had appeared in my path. I was given the opportunity to learn from them and see how things worked from small businesses to big corporates. I was also given glimpses in to the lives and the mindsets of very successful people who made things work and those that didn't and most importantly I was given the insight that these were all things I could achieve for myself if I put my mind to it. The main thing all these people had in common that set them apart from most others was their belief in themselves and an unfaltering determination they would do it their way... obviously they were talented and have specific skills, but if they can do it, I can find my way too.

Once my mind had decided that was it, I would run my own business and there were no options left, there was no stopping me and everything fell into place. The first idea I had I wanted a smoothie business that I could develop, so I googled 'smoothie shops for sale' and incredibly there were only two for sale in the entire UK and one was in my hometown and turned out to be the perfect unique opportunity! It was actually a very small milkshake shop that sold a few smoothies, but I knew instantly I had to have it. So, as simple as it sounds, I found a milkshake shop, thought 'I can do that', I bought it, put my life and soul in to it for over five years with ups and downs, but actually I've found all the things I was looking for. I have created a strong brand I am proud of, opened further stores, I have food outlets using my branding and products, I am working with charities and communities, have so many exciting plans for the future and much bigger dreams. I love what I do and, even better, I've had no strange homesickness feeling since 2015!

So, although I'm still in the process of making everything happen, I realised I'm a mixture of lots of different roles but they don't even matter and I'm just on a journey, which is magically unfolding. My mistake previously was trying to make myself happy based on what job title you have, the company you work for, location you're based, role you have and so on, but actually the most fulfilling thing for me is the freedom I have got from working for myself. I choose how I do things and create how I want my life and get enormous satisfaction from the relationships I have with the people around me. One of the most liberating feelings is that you don't have to 'be' anything at all you can just create the things and life you want by incorporating all the different parts of the things you have learnt and loved.

My main message to anyone reading this is if you also have that feeling that you are here for something extraordinary too, don't settle for less, keep moving forward. It is okay not to know how you will achieve it but, if you want to find true happiness, my advice is you work and create your dreams for yourself!

★★★

You can find Laura here:

https://www.instagram.com/shakes2go/
http://linkedin.com/in/laura-griffiths-4457a24b
https://www.instagram.com/lauracgriffiths/

# Your Past Doesn't Define You – It Refines You

## Lindsay Bentham

*Dedicated to my mum, my brother Paul, and my best friends Caroline and Kirsty.*

How do you tell your mum that you were sexually abused throughout your childhood? There never was a right time to voice it. I desperately wanted to tell her, I trusted her and loved her so much, yet I was terrified to let the words come out of my mouth. What if she didn't believe me, what damage would it do to the family? What if I was rejected? What would everybody think and say?

There were too many "what ifs". I was already carrying a huge amount of shame and guilt to start with, I couldn't take any chances, so I decided from a young age I wouldn't tell anyone. Nobody needed to know, so I decided the best option overall for everyone, including me, was to stay silent.

I buried that secret deep inside and vowed never to open it and I would carry on through life as if it never happened. My secret would die with me.

THE ELEVATION OF THE *Femalepreneur*

I mastered the skill from early adulthood to block out the horrible images from my mind. I disconnected from my emotions and built a wall of armour around me for protection from others. I didn't trust anyone, especially men.

Becoming a single mum of two young children in my mid-thirties, I found it increasingly hard to juggle the dynamics of a work-life balance on my own. There seemed to be a constant flow of challenging times; the more I tried to hold everything together, the quicker my life was crumbling around me. Unable to cope, I fell into depression. In my eyes, I was a failure, I was completely broken and defeated.

The flashbacks of my childhood abuse would catch me off guard, they reinforced my beliefs of being damaged goods and worthless. My inner critic took over my thoughts and I was at the lowest point in my life.

I didn't plan on telling my mum that day. I broke her heart. Hearing her gasp of sheer horror when I revealed who my abuser was, my emotions completely engulfed me. My heart was racing, body tense with fear, I began hitting the sides of my head with my fists and pulling at my hair to get the images out of my head. I hated myself, I hated being robbed of my childhood and I hated him.

I braced for the rejection. Huge relief came over me when my mum wrapped her arms around me and consoled me. I embraced that moment. I felt like a small child being saved.

I've always had a close bond with my mum and my oldest brother. I needed him too, so my mum contacted him and he came straight to my house unbeknown to him what news he was to hear. As soon as I saw him, I sobbed uncontrollably. I knew at that point when he hugged me tightly that I was safe.

My secret was out.

Reporting it to the police would be a challenging decision. Could I cope with the added stress to my depression? I knew deep down I had to report it, but it raised more "what ifs".

What if they didn't believe me? It was historic sexual abuse, after all, and I had no evidence – it was my word against his.

What if it goes to court? I'll be terrified, I'm not strong enough to cope, other people will find out and what will they think and say about it?

All this was whirring around in my head. I couldn't think straight, I was starting to panic.

Hearing my mum and brother would support me, whatever decision I decided to make next, was so reassuring. They believed me 100% and that was the most important thing to me.

I knew deep down I had to report it.

I called 999.

The police dealing with my case were so supportive, especially the assigned detective constable, Kirsty. She came to visit me over the next few days, and it took hours giving statements of each sexual abuse event. I had never disclosed my abuse to anyone in thirty-two years. I was distraught reliving each event, it brought up so many supressed emotions it overwhelmed me at times.

We developed a close bond over time, I trusted her, she believed me, and she was on my side.

During the next few months, I had a lot of therapy sessions. I needed it. It was difficult opening up. At times I didn't want to go back to being a child, the memories were too raw, and I couldn't cope with the emotional aftermath that would drain me for days after each session.

Slowly, I began unwrapping the layers of shame, guilt and hatred I had for myself. Years of stuck emotions started to unravel but I had a long way to go. I was only scratching the surface.

It took nearly two years for the case to be brought to court. Crown court. Once the date had been confirmed, I began to panic. The flashbacks came back with a vengeance, the recurring nightmares I had as a child returned and I took a lot of time off work, unable to concentrate. Completing the simplest of tasks at home took its toll and I withdrew from others and shut myself away.

That was my safety mechanism, isolating myself. My learned behaviour was to always stay silent, bottle my feelings and not communicate truthfully. I didn't want to be a burden to anyone with my trauma, so I'd pretend I was okay, but inside I felt I was dying. I was so afraid to stand up in a courtroom full of people, give evidence, be questioned and judged. I'd be faced with all my fears at the same time, and I was a complete wreck inside.

Writing my victim impact statement was one of the hardest things to complete, it took me forever to write. This was the turning point for me, it gave me strength to soldier on. I'd come this far, and I wasn't going to give up and continue hiding away. Seeing how much the abuse had affected my life and me as a person was a huge wake up call. It had profound effects throughout my life. My innocence had been stolen, shy and inward as a child, self-confidence and worth completely shattered, distrust in others and, most of all, my dignity taken.

No matter how difficult the court case would be and regardless of what the outcome was, I needed to see this through, in order to grow and rebuild my life. I was in control.

The court case was a one-week trial. I was to take the stand first. I hardly slept the night before. We were given a private room in the protection suite and I was on edge. My mum, brother and best friend were with me. I felt guilty having to put my mum and brother in a situation where they'd have to take the stand too. They were the first people I confessed to, so they had a role to play as well. We were all apprehensive and nervous and you could feel the tension in the air. I was on high alert every time I heard footsteps outside the room or a door opening, waiting for me to be called.

I debated over having a screen around me in the courtroom, to block out my abuser watching me. I didn't want to look at him but knowing he would be looking at me made my skin crawl and I needed to stay 100% focused. Court broke for lunch, so we decided to go to the restaurant and stretch our legs. Standing waiting to be served, my abuser walked in. I completely froze, but not in fear. It was an awful feeling of wanting to escape but my body wouldn't move. I couldn't even find my voice to alert my mum and friend that he was standing just a few feet behind me. I left and headed straight back to the private room. I told my brother what had just happened and within seconds something shifted inside me. I am not having a screen! I'm not hiding away any longer. I'll look him in the eyes and I'll tell the truth about exactly what he did to me. I felt courageous.

At 2pm I was eventually called. I sat outside the courtroom, maybe just for a few minutes but it seemed forever. My body was trembling, my heart racing and I tried to focus on my breathing. I was so anxious I remember clutching my friend's hand tightly; we looked at each other as my name was called and another shift inside me happened. "Let's do this!"

I'd never been in a courtroom before. Seeing the judge, the jury and barristers, I scanned the room to the public gallery, and I was relieved to see there were no reporters there.

I was questioned for two whole hours.

Back in the protection suite, seeing my mum and brother again, I broke down. A huge relief that my interrogation was over but then immediately panic set in. They don't believe me! None of the jury believe me! Not one of them would have eye contact with me! Not one.

I was no longer in control and I was distraught.

As the week unfolded and everyone gave their evidence, it was now my abuser's turn to take the stand.

Listening to him being interrogated and cross-examined gave me so much strength. Although he denied the abuse, seeing him scared and vulnerable was like sweet revenge. Karma at its finest.

Friday was judgement day. I decided to stay at home and Kirsty would call me with the outcome. I was on tenterhooks all day. I reran everything in my mind – did I do enough? And, of course, the "what ifs" raised their heads. I knew there was a chance he could walk free, and I was prepared for that possible outcome. I kept telling myself the reasons for speaking out were to save my own sanity, I needed to heal from the abuse and above all HE had to be held accountable for what he did to me.

The phone rang.

Kirsty broke the news: after only twelve minutes the jury found him guilty on all seventeen counts and he'd been immediately remanded. He'd be sentenced in four weeks' time. I was overwhelmed with mixed emotions, relief my nightmare was nearly over and, above all, "I was believed! The jury believed me!"

The following month came round quickly, I was back in the courtroom ready to read out my impact statement to the judge and I was nervous. Seeing his face on the prison video link made me want to vomit, but I was determined I'd never let him control me or my thoughts anymore. This was my last challenge, I composed myself, took a deep breath and read out my statement.

Watching the colour drain from his face when the judge sentenced him to nine and a half years was priceless. The amount of time he'd serve didn't matter to me, justice had been served and he was where he belonged.

I was so proud of myself; the feeling of empowerment was euphoric. I was so grateful to everyone who supported me 100%, especially my mum, Paul, Caroline and Kirsty. They were behind me every step of the way.

I naively assumed that by being free from secrets and speaking my truth I'd sail through life being happy and carefree. I found it hard slotting back into my old life, I didn't want to be juggling at life and being unfulfilled. Having spent thirty years living behind a mask of pretence I now wanted to embrace my new-found freedom and uncover the real Lindsay on the way, but I felt stuck. My self-confidence was low, I had so many limiting beliefs that were preventing me from moving forward.

I had to get my foundations right. My mindset! I delved into self-help books, spent hours listening to motivational podcasts and attended a Tony Robbins event searching for guidance.

I found a mindset coach and mentor who also specialises in healing from trauma. I've gone through lots of timeline therapy and I've done heaps of inner work. I have now been able to slowly unravel the stuck emotions I've held on to for so long.

My next aim is to focus on growing my Avon team so I can leave my main job. I've set a goal to complete this within the next twelve months. Working from home and around my family will give me more time freedom to fulfil my ambition of becoming a mentor myself.

Helping others to overcome childhood sexual abuse would be absolutely amazing.

It has been a long road of recovery for me, but I know I'm on the right path and I will succeed.

I used to be deeply ashamed of my past, but now I can proudly hold my head up high and say that: "My past didn't define me – it refined me!"

★★★

You can find Lindsay here:

https://www.facebook.com/profile.<br>php?id=100006037668124

# The Femalepreneur Academy

You see? You really can get through the tough times. Every single curveball thrown at us femalepreneurs, however big or small, we got through it and still kept chasing our dreams! We had a choice. To either give up on everything and let our past, our scars, whether physical or emotional, define us and hold us back forever, or we could stand back up after every hit and come back that little bit stronger every single time! We will keep rising from the darkness and allow our lights to shine through and be a beacon of hope to anyone out there who truly needs it.

So, if like any of us, there's been pain, hurt, trauma and fear, find the courage from within to push through it and be the femalepreneur you have always been destined to be. Your future self will thank you for it!

This is *The Elevation of the Femalepreneur*, and we will continue to rise together!

If any of these authors have resonated with you today, then be sure to reach out to them through their socials and connect!

If you'd like to know more about The Femalepreneurs Academy, you can find everything out about us by visiting www.femalepreneursacademyltd.com and if you have your own story to share, get in touch to apply for Volume four!

Love and light,
Your Femalepreneurs xoxo

Printed in Great Britain
by Amazon